SMITHSONIAN

Did You Know?

Earth

SMITHSONIAN
INSTITUTION

Established in 1846, the Smithsonian Institution—the world's largest museum and research complex—includes 19 museums and galleries and the National Zoological Park. The total number of artifacts, works of art, and specimens in the Smithsonian's collection is estimated at 155.5 million, the bulk of which is contained in the National Museum of Natural History, which holds more than 126 million specimens and objects. The Smithsonian is a renowned research center, dedicated to public education, national service, and scholarship in the arts, sciences, and history.

SMITHSONIAN

Did You Know?

Earth

Dr. Devin Dennie

Author Dr. Devin Dennie
Consultants Jonathan Dale, Prof. David M. Schultz,
Prof. Richard Worden
Smithsonian consultants Michael R. Ackerson, Ph.D.,
Research Geologist- Curator, Department of Mineral Sciences,
National Museum of Natural History, Smithsonian
Gabriela A. Farfan, Ph.D., Coralyn Whitney Curator of Gems
and Minerals, Department of Mineral Sciences,
National Museum of Natural History, Smithsonian
Illustrator Dan Crisp

DK LONDON
Editor Kathleen Teece, Manisha Majithia
Senior designer Fiona Macdonald, Ann Cannings
US Senior editor Shannon Beatty
US Editor Elizabeth Searcy
Additional editing Olivia Stanford, Katie Lawrence
Managing editor Laura Gilbert, Jonathan Melmoth
Managing art editor Diane Peyton Jones
Pre-production producer Nikoleta Parasaki, Abi Maxwell
Producer Isabell Schart, Magdalena Bojko
Deputy art director Mabel Chan
Publishing director Sarah Larter

DK DELHI
Editors Anwesha Dutta, Shambhavi Thatte
Designers Kartik Gera, Shipra Jain, Jaileen Kaur,
Nidhi Mehra, Nehal Verma, Mohd Zishan
Managing editor Alka Thakur Hazarika
Managing art editor Romi Chakraborty
DTP designers Mohammad Rizwan, Dheeraj Singh
CTS manager Balwant Singh
Production manager Pankaj Sharma
Picture researcher Aditya Katyal

This American Edition, 2022
First American Edition, 2019
Published in the United States by DK Publishing
345 Hudson Street, New York, New York 10014

Copyright © 2019, 2022 Dorling Kindersley Limited
DK, a Division of Penguin Random House LLC
19 20 21 22 23 10 9 8 7 6 5 4 3 2 1
001–327023–Sept/2022

A catalog record for this book
is available from the Library of Congress.
ISBN: 978-0-7440-5662-4

DK books are available at special discounts when purchased
in bulk for sales promotions, premiums, fund-raising, or
educational use. For details, contact: DK Publishing Special
Markets, 345 Hudson Street, New York, New York 10014
SpecialSales@dk.com

Printed and bound in China

For the curious
www.dk.com

MIX
Paper | Supporting
responsible forestry
FSC™ C018179

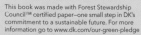
This book was made with Forest Stewardship
Council™ certified paper—one small step in DK's
commitment to a sustainable future. For more
information go to www.dk.com/our-green-pledge

SMITHSONIAN

Contents

Our planet

The Earth's surface

Blue planet

Up in the air

Living on the Earth

Find out why I became extinct on page 112.

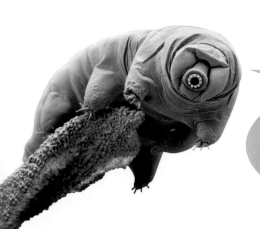

Discover which tiny creatures are hidden in moss on page 60.

Our planet

We are floating in space on a rocky planet called Earth. It is part of an eight-planet solar system that circles the sun (a star). Earth is just the right distance from the sun for life to exist, which makes our planet unique.

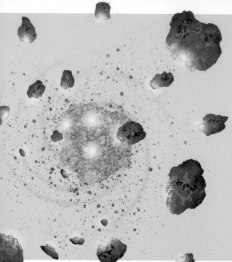

Space debris

Rocks, gas, and lumps of dirty ice once filled the space where the Earth would form. Around 4.6 billion years ago, a force called gravity began to pull the pieces together to form a mini planet called a planetoid.

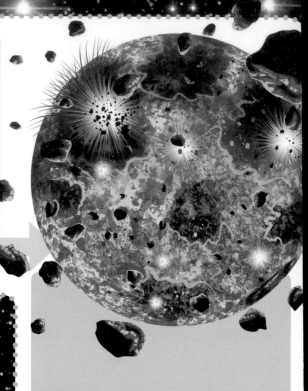

The growing Earth

Over millions of years, the Earth grew as more debris smashed into it. The explosive impacts caused the Earth's surface to melt. Heavy metals sank to the center to form the Earth's core.

How did the Earth form?

The Earth was once space dust. The sun came into existence about 4.6 billion years ago. It pulled gas, ice, and rocks into a disc around it. This spinning rubble collided to form the planets in our solar system, including the Earth.

Is the Earth round?

The Earth is round but not a true sphere. It is slightly egg shaped! This is because the Earth rotates. The strong force of the rotation makes it bulge out in the middle.

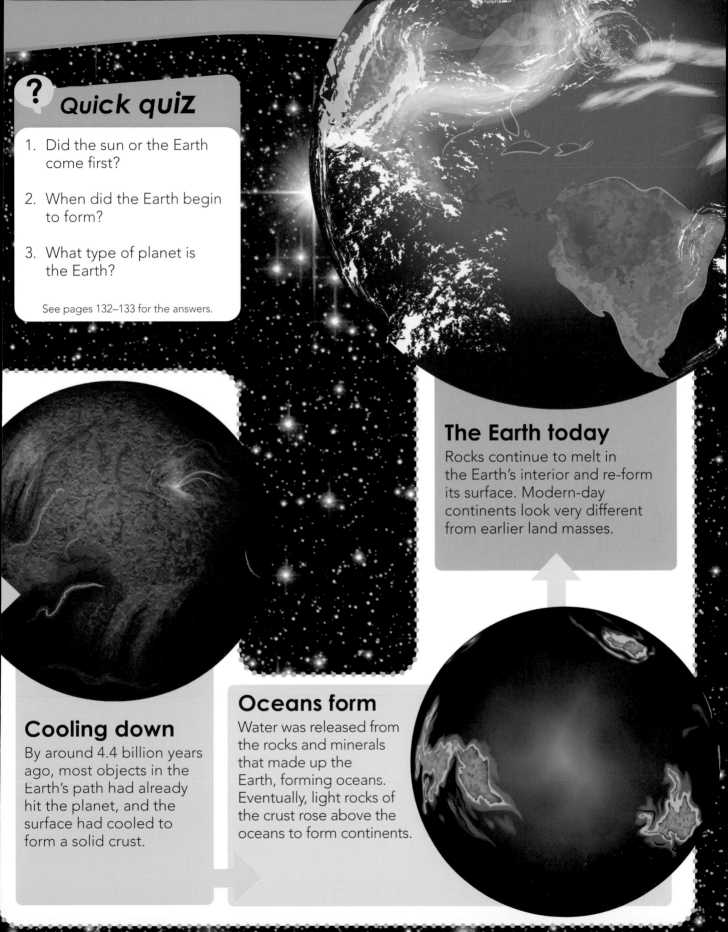

? Quick quiz

1. Did the sun or the Earth come first?

2. When did the Earth begin to form?

3. What type of planet is the Earth?

See pages 132–133 for the answers.

The Earth today

Rocks continue to melt in the Earth's interior and re-form its surface. Modern-day continents look very different from earlier land masses.

Cooling down

By around 4.4 billion years ago, most objects in the Earth's path had already hit the planet, and the surface had cooled to form a solid crust.

Oceans form

Water was released from the rocks and minerals that made up the Earth, forming oceans. Eventually, light rocks of the crust rose above the oceans to form continents.

Sun

How hot is the sun?

The corona is the outermost layer of the sun's atmosphere. It can reach around 3.1 million °F (1.7 million °C). The inner core is even hotter. Here, temperatures can soar to 28.8 million °F (16 million °C).

Space begins at the Kármán line, 62 miles (100 km) above the Earth.

How does the atmosphere keep us safe?

The Earth's layered atmosphere is like a protective blanket. It keeps us warm, gives us gas to breathe, and blocks the sun's harmful radiation. The Earth would be hit by more space rocks if they didn't burn up as they fell through the atmosphere.

Exosphere

This zone is just before outer space. Satellites and the International Space Station are found here. It starts at around 372 miles (600 km) above the Earth.

Thermosphere

Here, temperatures can get very high because gas particles absorb lots of the sun's energy.

Mesosphere

Meteors get hot and burn up by rubbing against the many gas particles in this layer.

Stratosphere

This zone contains a layer of ozone gas that absorbs harmful ultraviolet radiation coming from the sun.

Troposphere

Most weather happens in the lowest layer of the atmosphere. It reaches to about 12.4 miles (20 km) high.

Karman line

Ozone layer

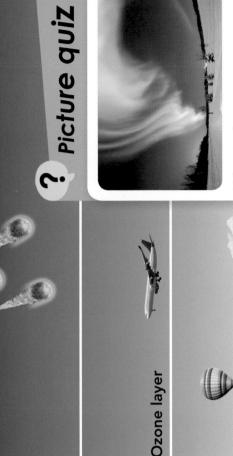

? Picture quiz

What is the common name of this light show that takes place in the atmosphere?

See pages 132–133 for the answer.

Third planet from the sun

Earth is a warm, rocky planet close to the sun, coming after Mercury and Venus. The furthermost planet, Neptune, is 2.7 billion miles (4.3 billion km) from Earth!

Sun   Mercury   Venus   Earth   Mars   Jupiter   Saturn   Uranus   Neptune

Hidden sun

The sun still shines at night—but on the other side of the Earth! Our planet blocks out the light.

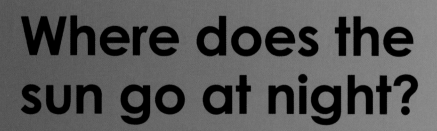

The Earth's axis

The Earth spins around an imaginary line called an axis. This line runs between the two poles.

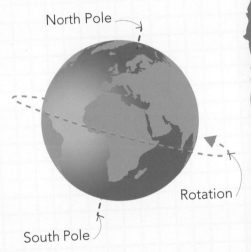

North Pole

Rotation

South Pole

The Earth spins on its axis.

The Earth

The Earth rotates in space, spinning like a top as it revolves around the sun.

Where does the sun go at night?

The sun doesn't go anywhere! The reason you can't see it at night is because the Earth spins. As the day passes, your country turns to face the opposite direction of the sun.

? Quick quiz

1. What is a meteorite?

2. Does the sun move around the Earth?

See pages 132–133 for the answers.

Visible sun

You can see the sun when your side of the Earth is facing it. Sometimes, the moon moves to block the sun. This is an eclipse.

The sun

The sun is our nearest star. It is huge and very hot inside. It gives out light and heat.

Light from the sun

Light from the sun travels through space to the Earth. This gives us daylight.

What are shooting stars?

Meteor

These are bodies of rock or ice in space. They were left over from the formation of the solar system, 4.6 billion years ago. Some "shooting stars" are no bigger than a grain of sand!

Meteorite

When a larger meteor falls to the Earth in one piece, the rock we find is called a meteorite.

How is the Earth like an onion?

Both the Earth and onions have layers! Heavy rocks and metals sink down inside the Earth, and lighter material rises. This creates layers of metal and rock. Heat and pressure deeper within the Earth cause some layers to melt.

Onion

Onions grow layer by layer. Like the Earth, these layers get thinner as they get closer to the surface.

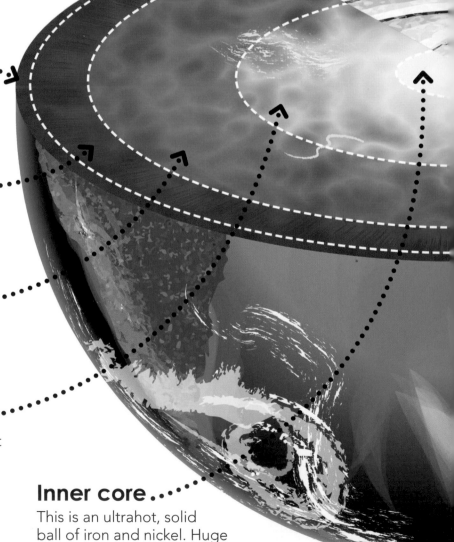

Crust

This is the solid outer layer made up of cold rocks. It is brittle and can break like toffee. Earth's crust is in pieces that fit together like a jigsaw.

Upper mantle

This warm layer has lower pressure than the layers beneath. Its upper portions flow slowly, like toothpaste.

Lower mantle

This rigid layer of hot rock is under so much pressure from outer layers that it can't melt or flow.

Outer core

This metallic zone is so hot that it melts into liquid. The metal spins around the Earth's inner core.

Inner core

This is an ultrahot, solid ball of iron and nickel. Huge pressure stops it from melting.

Types of crust

There are two types of crust. Oceanic crust beneath oceans is thin and dense. Continental crust is thicker and less dense. It is lighter than oceanic crust.

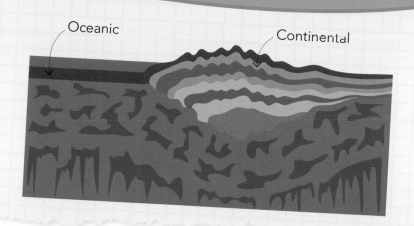

Oceanic

Continental

How far down have humans dug?

The Kola Superdeep Borehole in the Kola Peninsula in Russia is the deepest well ever drilled. It is 7.5 miles (12 km) deep. This is over 15 times the height of the Burj Khalifa in Dubai, the tallest building in the world!

Kola Superdeep Borehole

15 Burj Khalifas

? Quick quiz

1. Is the inner core of the Earth solid?

2. How much of Earth's surface is formed of oceanic crust?

3. Is the Earth's crust all in one piece?

See pages 132–133 for the answers.

Why don't things float off the Earth?

A force called gravity keeps us stuck to the Earth. This force pulls objects toward each other. The sun's gravity keeps the Earth in orbit around it. Without the Earth's gravity, we'd all float away!

Weaker pull

All objects pull things toward them using gravity, but the force is much weaker for small objects.

Is there gravity everywhere in space?

The Earth's neighborhood

The Earth's gravity pulls spacecraft toward it, but there is no atmosphere in space to slow them down, so the spacecraft keep moving. This keeps them orbiting around the planet rather than falling to its surface.

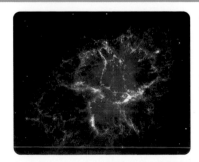

Outer space

Even in the farthest reaches of space there is gravity. The gravity of far-off stars spreads out around them for massive distances.

? *True or false?*

1. The sun pulls the Earth toward it with gravity.

2. Dogs have a tiny force of gravity.

3. There is no gravity in outer space.

See pages 132–133 for the answers.

Orbital gravity

Gravity from large objects in space pulls other objects into oval-shaped paths called orbits. The objects keep moving but can't escape the pull.

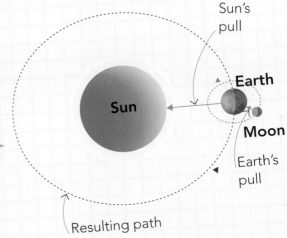

Sun's pull

Earth

Sun

Moon

Earth's pull

Resulting path

The Earth's gravity

Gravity is stronger the nearer an object is. When you stand right on the Earth's surface, you experience maximum gravity.

Why can't we live on Mars?

Humans need liquid water and air with lots of oxygen to survive. The only planet where these are found is Earth. Some scientists are planning a human-made colony on Mars, but we couldn't live outside on the freezing, low-oxygen surface.

Goldilocks zone

The Earth is neither too hot nor too cold, like the porridge in "Goldilocks and the Three Bears." Water here doesn't all freeze or turn to steam, so plants can grow. These plants make oxygen for us to breathe.

Too hot

As the closest planets to the sun, Mercury and Venus are just too hot. Gases in Venus's atmosphere trap the heat to make it even hotter. The lack of gas on Mercury makes it freezing at night.

Mercury

Venus

Sun

The sun makes energy that hits planets as light and creates heat. Each planet gets a different amount of energy.

Earth

Too cold

Mars is too cold because of its distance from the sun. The only water here is frozen at the poles or underground.

Mars

Are there other habitable planets?

There are billions of planets in the universe. We have recently found ones that may be similar to Earth, such as Kepler-62f.

? Picture quiz

Which planet comes after Mars?

See pages 132–133 for the answer.

Did the chicken or the egg come first?

The first ever chicken hatched out of an egg laid by an earlier species! Life on the Earth faces many challenges. Over time, babies with features that help them better survive are born and flourish. This process is called evolution.

Chickens eat stones to help them grind down food in their gizzards. Dinosaurs had gizzards too!

Dinosaur egg

Dinosaurs hatched out of eggs just like birds do. This is because birds evolved from dinosaurs.

Fluffy feathers

Both velociraptors and chickens evolved from the same unknown dinosaur. Despite being much bigger than chickens, velociraptors had feathers, like birds.

How do we know about evolution?

DNA
What we look like depends on our DNA. When species have similar DNA, it shows that they are related.

Fossil
Fossils are remains of ancient creatures. They can tell us how animals have evolved from those of ancient times.

Penguin
Penguins evolved to survive in harsh Antarctic conditions. They developed waterproof feathers that keep them warm and allow them to swim rather than fly.

Quick quiz

1. How old are the remains of the oldest bacteria?

2. Are crocodiles related to dinosaurs?

3. When did dinosaurs become extinct?

See pages 132–133 for the answers.

First life on the Earth
Single-celled life, like bacteria, were the first living things. Scientists think that the earliest signs of life may have emerged around 4 billion years ago.

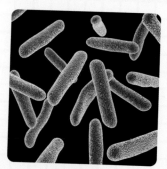

Bacteria

Dinosaur descendants
A huge extinction event wiped out most of the dinosaurs 65 million years ago. Some small descendants survived and evolved into birds.

Terrifying talons
Birds such as chickens have many dinosaur-like features. They have light, hollow skeletons, similar lungs and hearts, and talons!

Does land stay still?

The Earth's surface is always moving but usually so slowly that we can't feel it. In the past, this motion caused the continents to collide, forming a supercontinent called Pangaea. The continents may collide again, many millions of years in the future.

Changing continents

Northern Pangaea became North America, Europe, and parts of Asia. Southern Pangaea broke up into South America, Africa, Australia, Antarctica, and India.

The seven continents today

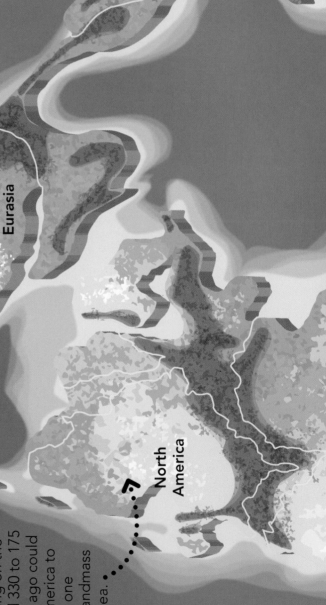

Eurasia

North America

Supercontinent

Creatures living on the Earth around 330 to 175 million years ago could walk from America to Africa across one continuous landmass called Pangaea.

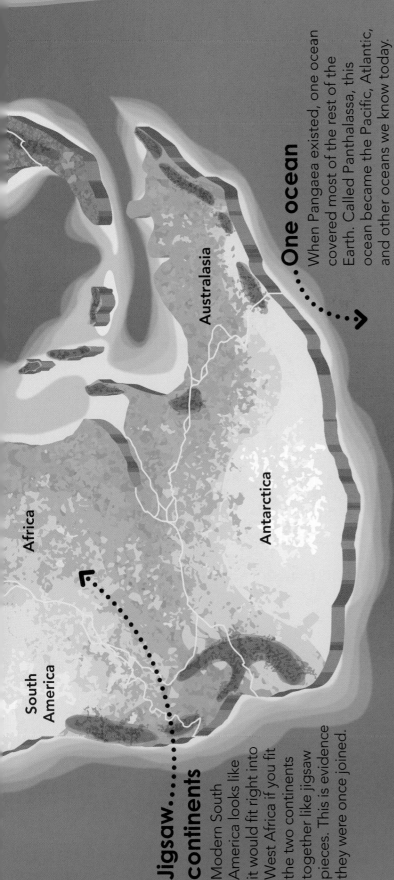

Jigsaw continents

Modern South America looks like it would fit right into West Africa if you fit the two continents together like jigsaw pieces. This is evidence they were once joined.

South America

Africa

Australasia

Antarctica

One ocean

When Pangaea existed, one ocean covered most of the Earth. Called Panthalassa, this ocean became the Pacific, Atlantic, and other oceans we know today.

What clues suggest that the continents were once joined together?

Dinosaur fossils

Similar dinosaur remains found on different continents suggest they could once walk from one continent to the other.

Plant fossils

Plants can't spread their seeds across oceans, so similar plant fossils found on separate continents suggest a once-connected land.

? Picture quiz

The remains of which African animal have been found in Derbyshire, England?

See pages 132–133 for the answer.

Did everywhere freeze in the last ice age?

An ice age occurs when the Earth gets colder and ice covers large parts of it. The most recent ice age lasted from around 118,000 BCE to 10,000 BCE. Many of today's cities would have been under ice, but the warm equator stayed mostly ice-free.

Last ice age
Over the 100,000 years that made up the last ice age, huge ice sheets, or glaciers, covered many places where there are now cities.

North America
The places where New York and other northern US cities are today were once under ice thick enough to cover the world's tallest skyscrapers.

South America
What is now Caracas in Venezuela and most of the rest of South America were too warm for ice to form.

Can woolly mammoths come back to life?

A chemical in animals' bodies called DNA contains instructions on how the animals first formed. The DNA of an extinct mammoth frozen in ice is being studied in order to possibly re-create this huge animal.

The Arctic

The Arctic was a thick and massive ice sheet in the last ice age. Today, many parts are still locked in ice.

Europe

The places that would become Warsaw and other northern European cities were under ice. Southern city sites were cool but without ice.

Africa

What is now Nouakchott in Mauritania and many other parts of Africa are near the equator. Places such as this would have been ice-free.

? Quick quiz

1. How thick did ice sheets get during the last ice age?

2. When did the last ice age end?

3. Was the place where New York City is today once under ice?

See pages 132–133 for the answers.

Interglacial

The periods of melting between ice ages are called interglacial. Today, we are in an interglacial period. It is warmer and most of the glaciers from the last ice age have melted.

The Earth's surface

The Earth's surface is always changing. Water, wind, and ice wear down its rocks and soil to create new and wonderful landforms. Heat deep inside the Earth melts rock, turning it into lava that erupts from volcanoes and magma from which whole continents form.

Do mountains grow?

Some mountains are getting bigger, but you'd have to watch one for a long time to see it grow! Underground, the Earth is divided into moving rocky segments, or tectonic plates. These plates collide, or bump into each other, and push each other up into mountain ranges, such as the Himalayas.

Young mountains

The Himalayas are relatively young mountains. Some mountain ranges are over a billion years old.

How did the Himalayas form?

The Himalayas formed around 40 to 50 million years ago, when the continental plate beneath India crashed into the Eurasian plate.

The plates collide.

The mountains are pushed up farther.

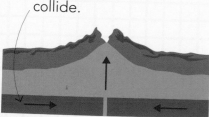

Collision

When India crashed into the southern edge of Eurasia, the rock was forced up and out of the ground.

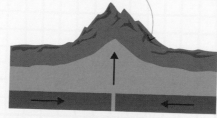

Growing mountains

The plates are still slowly pushing against each other today, so the mountains continue to rise.

Rising peaks

The Himalayan peaks grow by about 0.2 in (5 mm) every year.

Wall of mountains

Young mountain ranges are essentially straight, flat walls of rock because water and wind haven't worn them down very much.

? ## True or false?

1. Mauna Kea was formed by plates colliding.

2. Mountains grow over time.

3. The Himalayas are the oldest mountain range in the world.

See pages 132–133 for the answers

How else do mountains form?

Mountains can also form from volcanoes. Over time, molten rock called lava erupts out of the volcano and hardens to form igneous rock. This rock can build up and become high volcanic mountains, such as Mauna Kea in Hawaii.

Are volcanic flows slow or fast?

You could outwalk or outrun most lava flows. However, not all eruptions are the same. Some lava streams can flow up to 40 mph (64 kph), while others may explode violently!

Lava

Magma that erupts above ground is called lava. Thick and very hot lava flows slowly. Cooler, lighter lava containing gas may explode into columns of ash.

Eruption

Molten rock called magma is found deep underground. It can rise up and erupt through fissures (cracks) in the ground. As each layer of lava cools, it can form a steep stratovolcano that gets bigger with more eruptions.

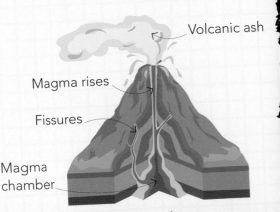

Volcanic ash

Magma rises

Fissures

Magma chamber

Stratovolcano

Are there different types of volcanoes?

Caldera
Calderas are large, cone-shaped depressions, often containing valleys or lakes. They are made when volcanoes collapse after the magma from underground chambers is released.

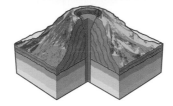

Cinder cone
These landforms are created when hot lava erupts out of the ground and hardens into cinders, or tiny pieces of rock. The cinders build up and form a cone.

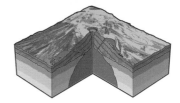

Shield
Shield volcanoes are made of stacks of hardened layers of lava. Mauna Loa, on the island of Hawaii, is a giant shield volcano.

Ash cloud
Burning material called ash erupts from volcanoes. Some superhot, gassy ash clouds can erupt at 200 mph (322 kph)!

? True or false?

1. The temperature of some lava is over 2,732 °F (1,500 °C).

2. Lava is rock.

See pages 132–133 for the answers.

What happens when water gets superheated?

Some water is found underground in chambers. Here, the water can get warmed to high temperatures by heat coming from deep inside the Earth. This hot water can find its way to the surface, creating a variety of unique landforms.

Steam

Superheated water deep underground boils and then turns into steam. This provides the energy for the geyser to erupt.

Porous rock

Surface water can seep down through holes and cracks in the layers of rock underground. The water is heated up by the Earth's hot interior.

What are the other features of natural hot water?

Hot springs

Hot springs are features where hot water emerges from the ground. The water is warmed underground by hot rocks.

Mud pots

When hot springs happen in areas with volcanic ash or mud, the water mixes with the mud or ash to form a thick, gloppy sludge. These features are called mud pots.

Geyser

Underground water rises quickly, spilling out at surface level. The steam pushes the rest of the water out in a powerful eruption.

High pressure

The geyser's narrow opening means water cannot easily escape. This causes pressure to build up in hollow pockets underground, eventually blasting the water and steam out.

? Quick quiz

1. What mixes with hot springs to form mud pots?

2. Where is the Earth's tallest geyser?

3. How high can water from the Steamboat Geyser reach?

See pages 132–133 for the answers.

Yellowstone National Park has more than 500 geysers, including Earth's tallest, Steamboat Geyser!

The front part of this geyser has been cut away to show the hot water inside.

Is soil made of animals?

Soil is a mixture of different materials, including animal remains! The makeup of soil depends on the types of rocks and plants in an area, as well as the climate, the angle of the ground, and how long the soil took to form.

Soil horizons

Soil can be divided into horizontal, or sideways, layers called horizons. These layers develop as surface materials are affected by air, water, and living things. Each layer was formed differently and has a unique soil type.

Minerals

Rocks are made of minerals, which are tiny crystals of natural material. When rocks break down, the minerals become part of the soil.

Animal remains

When animals die, their bodies break down into smaller pieces inside soil. This process is called decomposition.

? True or false?

1. The leaching layer is the top layer of soil.

2. Peat can be burned for heat and fossil-fuel energy.

3. Rain can wash away loose soil.

See pages 132–133 for the answers.

Sandy soil

Sand-sized soil grains can be up to 0.08 in (2 mm) big. There are spaces between the grains that allow the soil to store plenty of air and water.

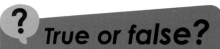

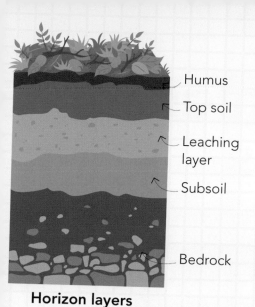

- Humus
- Top soil
- Leaching layer
- Subsoil
- Bedrock

Horizon layers

Why are soils in danger?

Soil can be washed away by rain. Tree roots help hold soil in place so that it isn't washed away. When trees are cut down for wood or to clear land, rain carries away the loose soil.

Earthworm

Worms help agitate, digest, and turn over soil, which helps break down plants quicker.

Peaty soil

Some soils are rich in broken-down plant materials called peat, which is found in marshes or bogs.

Void space

Air and water are stored in soil. This soil moisture is important for plants and for keeping soil stuck together.

Plants

Leaves and other dead parts of plants break down to become part of soil.

Do I contain minerals?

Minerals are natural solids found in our bones, the food we eat, and almost everything we see—from stainless steel to gemstones. Different kinds of minerals are made up of different chemical ingredients.

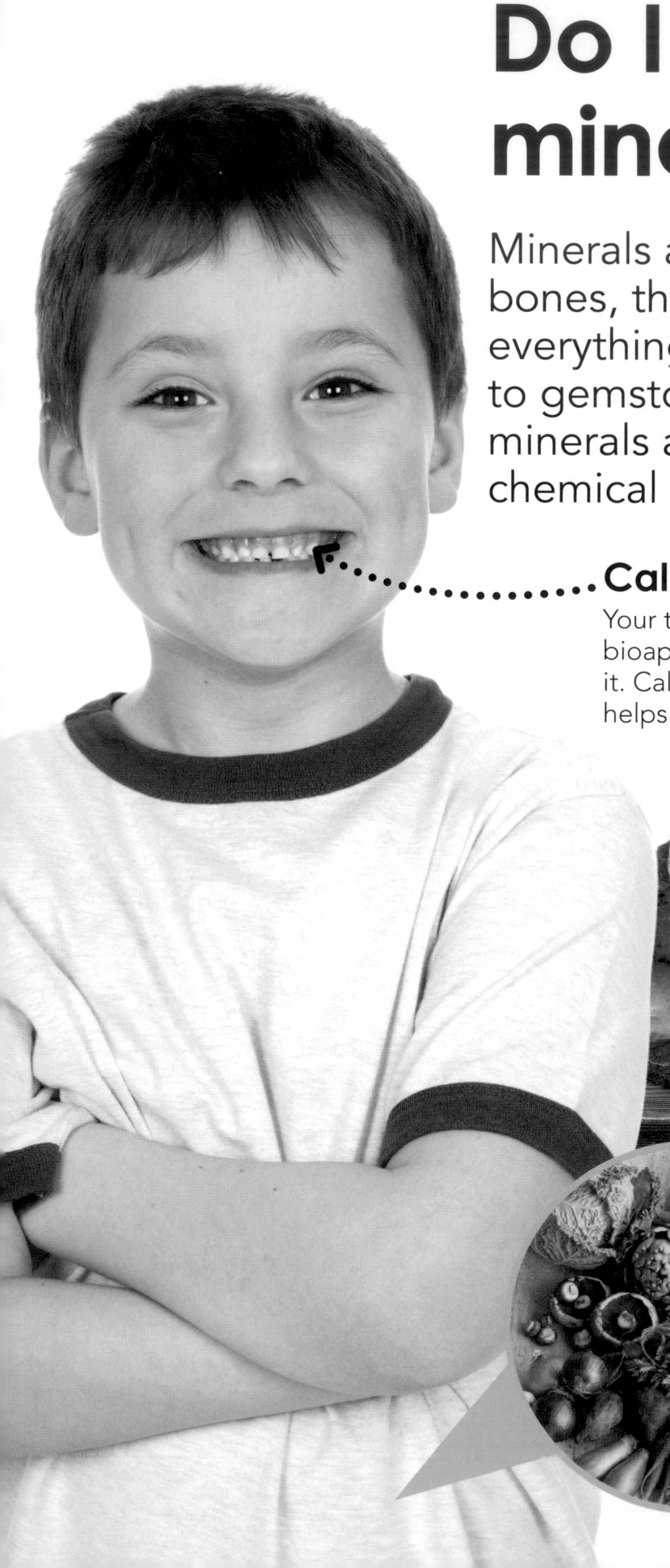

Calcium in teeth

Your teeth contain the mineral bioapatite, which has calcium in it. Calcium in our food and drinks helps make teeth strong.

Serpentine

Celestite

Sulfur

Vegetables

When vegetables grow, the roots of the plants take up nutrients from the minerals in soil. Plants also make minerals to help them grow bigger.

Crystal structure

Minerals grow in crystal shapes. The smallest part of an object is an atom. Crystal atoms are lined up neatly to make different geometric shapes.

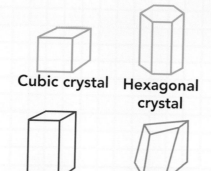

Cubic crystal

Hexagonal crystal

Tetragonal crystal

Triclinic crystal

Minerals

Gemstones and other minerals are made up of special crystal shapes. Different minerals have unique colors and textures.

Silicate mineral

Many minerals contain a natural material called silica. They are called silicates. A wide variety of minerals contain silica, including amethyst.

Rose quartz

Garnet

Opal

Amethyst

What are minerals used for?

Minerals have a variety of uses. Many types of toothpaste contain silica, which helps to rub your teeth clean. Medicines such as antacids, which help get rid of gas in your tummy, also contain minerals.

Which rock should I build with?

Rocks have been used for statues and as building blocks for thousands of years because of their hardness, toughness, and overall strength. Different types of rock have different levels of strength.

Which is the hardest mineral?

Rocks are made of minerals. The Mohs scale orders minerals by hardness, and diamond has the top ranking of 10! This makes it the hardest mineral. Diamonds are found underground or can be created by humans.

White marble

Marble is limestone that has been compressed deep underground. It is stronger than limestone because the minerals inside are more tightly packed.

Granite

Granite is one of the toughest stones on Earth. It's made up of hard minerals such as quartz and feldspar, making it strong.

Limestone and concrete

Limestone is made of a soft mineral called calcite. Nevertheless, it is the basis for concrete, one of the world's most important building materials. Concrete is not easily worn down, unlike natural limestone.

Bust of a man, Cyprus

Sedimentary rock

This type of rock is often softer and is worn away by weather more easily than other types of rock. It is made of compressed sediment, such as sand, or the remains of ancient plants and animals.

Bust of Venus, Italy

Metamorphic rock

This type of rock has been exposed to intense heat and pressure from being buried deep in the Earth.

Colossal granite head of Amenhotep III, Egypt

Igneous rock

Igneous rocks such as granite form from molten rock underground that has cooled and hardened. As the rocks grow, mineral crystals inside lock together to make the rocks very strong.

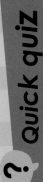

? Quick quiz

1. The Mohs scale measures
   a) Wetness
   b) Hardness
   c) Size

2. A metamorphic rock is a rock that has undergone
   a) Heat and pressure
   b) Being worn away by the weather
   c) Being cut by humans

See pages 132–133 for the answers.

Can a cliff turn into sand?

Cliffs might seem strong, but small fragments of rock are always breaking off. Water, wind, and ice grind down rock into sand. This process is called weathering. Parts of this canyon in Yellowstone National Park have been worn away over time.

Water in rock

In winter, the water contained in tiny holes and cracks inside rock freezes. This hard ice expands, breaking the rock into smaller pieces.

River

Flowing water picks up large rocks. The rocks break apart into smaller pieces as they roll and bounce along.

Wind

Strong winds can carry sand. The sand slowly scratches and sculpts rocks over time.

Why is sand different colors?

Sand varies in color based on the rocks it has broken down from. Black sand comes from eroded volcanic material, such as lava and other dark-colored rocks and minerals.

Sand

This sand was once part of larger rocks in the cliffs above. The rock was carried away and broken down by the river.

Quick quiz

1. When did the Yellowstone Canyon form?

2. What is the process that breaks down rock called?

3. Can humans wear rock down by walking on it?

See pages 132–133 for the answers.

Why do rocks form amazing shapes?

Water, wind, and ice transform our landscapes in a process called erosion. They create interesting landforms like the Wave, which cascades through a valley in Arizona.

Shaping rocks

Initially eroded by rainwater flowing over them millions of years ago, these sandstone rocks continued to be shaped by the force of strong winds.

How does water erosion happen?

Water carries sediment, made up of bits of rock, from one place to another. By removing pieces of rock, the water changes the shape of the rock left behind.

Water cuts through rock.

Sediment is carried by water.

What types of rocky landforms are there?

Natural bridge
These form when a stream or river erodes the lower part of a rock, leaving a natural bridge of rock above it.

Canyon
As erosion carries away sediment, a hollow called a canyon forms. Over millions of years, this process created the Grand Canyon.

Tower
These upright rock formations are what remain after a lot of erosion. Similar shapes include spires, hoodoos, and fairy chimneys.

Ancient dunes
The supercontinent containing what is now the United States once had vast areas of sand dunes, formed by wind. The Wave is what's left of some of them.

Varied colors
The colored stripes in this rock came from different minerals in wind-blown sand that settled in layers in an ancient sand dune.

? Quick quiz

1. What do the colors in the Wave show?

2. Which river wore away rocks to create the Grand Canyon?

3. What type of rock is the Wave made of?

See pages 132–133 for the answers.

Could I become a fossil?

Fossils are the rocky remains of plants and animals that lived long, long ago. The fossils most people think of are dinosaur bones, but many different kinds can be found. Even you could become a fossil one day, if you were buried deeply enough!

Coprolites are fossilized poop!

A fish dies and sinks to the ocean floor.

The bones are left when the rest of the body is eaten or decays.

The ocean begins to dry.

Sediment builds up.

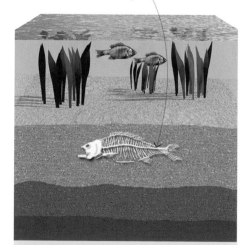

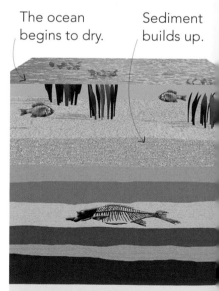

Death

Fossils start out as living things, such as fish. After death, soft parts of the body, such as skin and other organs, begin to be eaten away by worms or other fish.

Decay

The bones are left behind. They start to be covered by sediment, such as sand and mud. Over time, layers of sediment build up to cover the skeleton.

Rock forms

Sediment buries the skeleton deep underground. Fluids and the pressure of the ground pressing down transform the sediment and fish into new rock.

What are some other examples of fossils?

Molds
When living things die and rot away, they can leave the outline of their shapes, such as shells, in the ground. These are called molds.

Buried in amber
Amber is made of fossilized tree resin. Insects get caught in the sticky liquid, which hardens around them, preserving the body.

Fish and other marine animals are the most common fossils.

Scientists called paleontologists dig up fossils using tools.

Discovery
Millions of years later, the layer of rock becomes exposed at the surface through erosion or other processes. A fossil may then be discovered.

Body fossil
Different types of fossils have distinct shapes. Body fossils are bones or hard shells that have become rock. Trace fossils, such as footprints, record movements of living things.

The rock around fossils gives clues about the time when the organism lived.

Can you freeze in a desert?

Deserts are known for being smolderingly hot, but they also get so cold that a person might freeze! Deserts receive less than 10 in (25 cm) of rain each year. This means there isn't enough water in the air to hold heat once the sun goes down.

Cold desert

The Gobi Desert in Asia is cold all year round! It's still a desert because it has barely any wet weather. A dusting of snow might be carried by wind from Siberia, though.

Antarctica is the largest desert in the world. It covers an area of 5.5 million sq miles (14 million sq km)!

High altitude

Alpine deserts form where air is cold and thin and there isn't much precipitation, or rain and snow. Very little vegetation grows this high up.

Can living things survive in cold deserts?

Bactrian camel

Camels are animals built for dry desert living. They can go for months without drinking water and store excess fat for energy in their two large humps.

Saltwort

This grass can consume the salty water common in many deserts. Animals don't eat the salty plant, and its low freezing point means it can survive in low temperatures.

? True or false?

1. The coldest place on the Earth is at the top of Mount Everest.

2. Deserts are hot at night.

See pages 132–133 for the answers.

How does a sinkhole sink?

Certain types of rock can dissolve, or wear down, below the Earth's surface. This causes a void, or empty space. The surface can eventually sink inward into the void to form a sinkhole.

Formation of a sinkhole

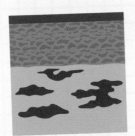

Acidic liquids can dissolve certain types of rock, such as limestone. Rainwater is slightly acidic and starts to dissolve some of the rock in the ground.

A cave forms as more and more rock is dissolved. The cave slowly enlarges. The roof of rock above gets thinner and starts to form cracks.

The roof of the cave eventually collapses. The cave is now exposed to the sky. It leaves a nearly circular hole in the Earth's surface—a sinkhole!

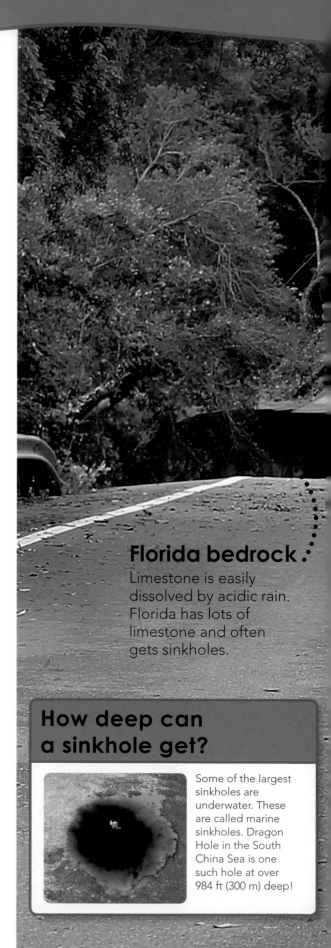

Florida bedrock

Limestone is easily dissolved by acidic rain. Florida has lots of limestone and often gets sinkholes.

How deep can a sinkhole get?

Some of the largest sinkholes are underwater. These are called marine sinkholes. Dragon Hole in the South China Sea is one such hole at over 984 ft (300 m) deep!

Ground caving in

Holes can form beneath the ground without people knowing. It's a total surprise when the ground collapses into a sinkhole!

Holey rock

Acidic rainwater dissolves some types of rock. This leaves holes in the rock and makes it weaker.

? Picture quiz

What caused the uneven land in Thailand?

See pages 132–133 for the answer.

How do raindrops make a cave?

When it rains, some of the carbon dioxide gas in the air dissolves in the raindrops. This makes the water slightly acidic. When the rain meets certain rocks, such as limestone, the water eats away at them, making a hole. These holes grow and become caves.

Stalactite

If water slowly drips from the ceiling of a cave over a long period, the minerals left behind from the water build up in a downward direction, creating a stalactite.

Stalagmite

When water drips onto the cave floor, minerals dissolved in the water can form solid deposits on the ground. These deposits grow upward over time, making pointed stalagmites.

Can caves form in other ways?

Weathering

Rocks can be broken up physically, such as when ice freezes and melts in fractures. This can remove softer rock from below a harder one, leaving a cave.

Lava tubes

Lava tubes form when molten rock cools into stone around its edges. The lava in the center remains hot, eventually flowing away and leaving a cave behind.

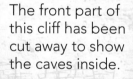

The front part of this cliff has been cut away to show the caves inside.

Column

If a stalactite and stalagmite meet, they fuse into a single pillar from floor to ceiling, called a column.

Fracture

Cracks or breaks in the ground, called fractures, let acidic water reach the rocks below.

? Quick quiz

1. Does a stalagmite grow from the floor or ceiling?

2. Is acid rain dangerous for humans?

3. What forms when a stalactite and stalagmite meet?

See pages 132–133 for the answers.

Cave pool

Underground rivers and streams continue to dissolve the rock around them, and sometimes water collects in pools.

China

The plate beneath China is bordered by the Pacific and Indian plates. These rub and push against each other, causing earthquakes.

Turkey

Turkey's Anatolian plate is caught between the larger Eurasian and African plates, which are squeezing and spinning Turkey!

Plate boundaries

The place where the edges of plates meet is called a plate boundary. Earthquakes often happen here.

Do earthquakes hit the same places?

Beneath the ground, the Earth's rocky crust is broken up into large pieces called tectonic plates. These plates constantly move and can rub against each other, pull apart, or collide, causing earthquakes.

United States

Earthquakes here happen mostly along the Pacific coast, where the North American plate slides past the Pacific one.

Ring of Fire

Many earthquakes take place along this long, narrow stretch of land and water surrounding the Pacific Ocean.

Chile

Here, the Nazca plate slides beneath the South American plate. The most powerful earthquake ever recorded took place in Chile in 1960.

? Quick quiz

1. How do ocean ridges form?

2. Which plate is caught between the Eurasian and African plates?

3. How many of the world's earthquakes take place along the Ring of Fire?

See pages 132–133 for the answers.

How do plates cause earthquakes?

Convergent

Plates collide. Volcanoes and mountains may form where continental and oceanic plates meet, or converge.

Transform

Plates slide past each other. When two plates rub against each other, it causes large earthquakes.

Divergent

Plates move apart. When this happens beneath oceans, molten rock rises up and forms the new sea floor.

Do islands float?

Islands don't really float—they just appear to! Islands are solidly attached to the ocean floor. They may form from the accumulation of coral reefs on the seabed. Some, called seamounts, are the tips of undersea volcanoes.

Island

An island is a piece of land surrounded on all sides by water. Islands are always smaller than continents.

How are volcanic islands formed?

Lava from underwater volcanoes hardens into rock. The rock accumulates in layers on the sides of the volcano. Eventually, the volcano peeps out of the sea.

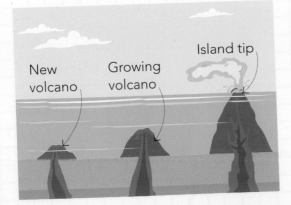

New volcano

Growing volcano

Island tip

Can you get floating rock islands?

One type of volcanic rock, pumice, is lighter than water, so it floats! Underwater volcanoes produce the rock, and rafts of it float, resembling islands.

? *True or false?*

1. A chain of islands is called an archipelago.

2. Pumice is the only known rock that floats in water.

See pages 132–133 for the answers.

Rock beneath
Islands are anchored to the ocean floor deep below by a column of rock.

Sinking island
Over time, island rocks of extinct volcanoes may erode away over time and become submerged in the ocean again.

Desert

This biome receives little or no rain. Here, tough plants and animals store water in their bodies and can cope with intense heat.

Dromedary camel

Saguaro cactus

Boreal forest, or taiga, is the largest biome on Earth. Almost 30 percent of the world's trees are found here.

Rainforest

Some rainforests get almost endless rain—up to 98 in (250 cm) a year! At least half of the plants and animals on Earth live here.

How is a cactus like a camel?

A camel and a cactus can both go a long time without water, helping them survive in their desert homes. Groups of living things with common features that help them cope in similar environments are called biomes.

Grassland

Wide, treeless grasslands have plants that are adapted to a range of seasonal climate changes.

Polar regions

Lands near the North Pole and South Pole are cold all year round and can be dry and lifeless. Life here is adapted to cold weather with little food.

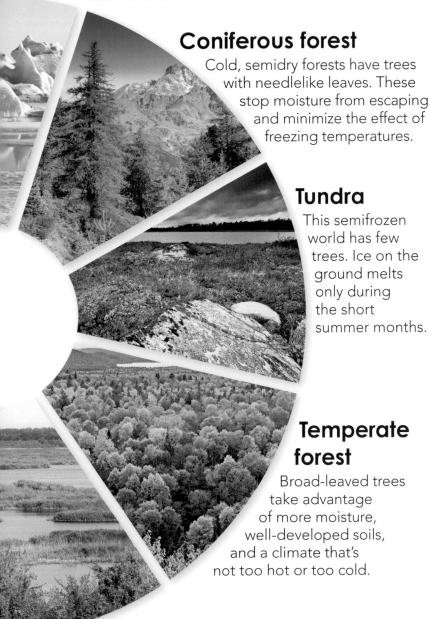

Coniferous forest

Cold, semidry forests have trees with needlelike leaves. These stop moisture from escaping and minimize the effect of freezing temperatures.

Tundra

This semifrozen world has few trees. Ice on the ground melts only during the short summer months.

Temperate forest

Broad-leaved trees take advantage of more moisture, well-developed soils, and a climate that's not too hot or too cold.

Wetlands

These areas are covered by water all or part of the time. Animals here must adapt to a watery life while also being able to live on land.

Are there other types of biomes?

Farmland

The only human-made biome, farmland is made up of areas specially adapted by people to grow crops or rear animals.

Marine biomes

Land makes up just 29 percent of the Earth's surface. The other 71 percent is oceans and other bodies of water, which we call marine biomes.

? Quick quiz

1. Which is the only human-made biome?

2. In which biome do camels live?

3. Which is the largest tropical rainforest in the world?

See pages 132–133 for the answers.

Do swamp monsters exist?

There are some weird and wonderful creatures in swamps. A swamp is a forest that is fully or partially submerged in water. Swamp creatures in Florida have special features for living in water.

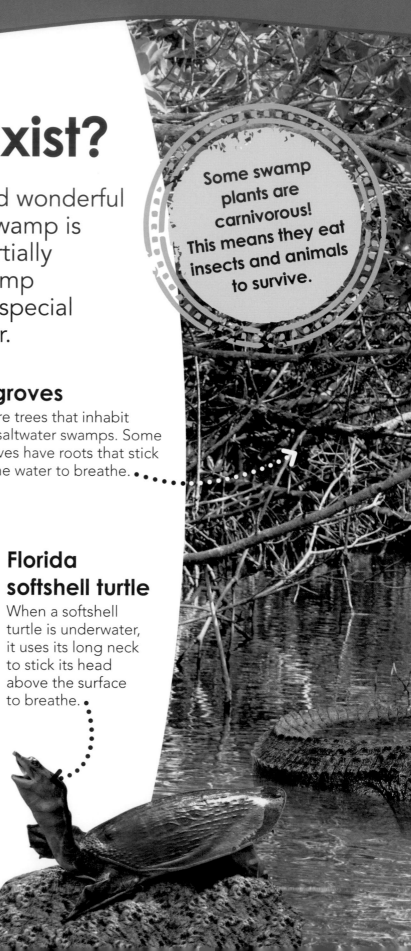

Some swamp plants are carnivorous! This means they eat insects and animals to survive.

Mangroves

These are trees that inhabit coastal saltwater swamps. Some mangroves have roots that stick out of the water to breathe.

Can people live in watery ecosystems?

People live in swamps by building houses on stilts. Many use fanboats to get around. These have aircraft-style propellers instead of underwater ones, which might get caught in shallow-water plants.

Florida softshell turtle

When a softshell turtle is underwater, it uses its long neck to stick its head above the surface to breathe.

West Indian manatee

Also called a "sea cow," this large animal grazes beneath the water in some swamps. It has flippers that help it swim through water.

? **True or false?**

1. A lesser siren is a type of eel.

2. Mangroves are also known as sea cows.

3. Alligators and crocodiles are the same animal.

See pages 132–133 for the answers.

American alligator

This reptile can grow up to 14 ft (4.3 m) long. An alligator can move quickly to drag prey underwater with its huge jaws.

Lesser siren

This looks like an eel but is actually a salamander. It has two legs and gills to breathe underwater like a fish!

Is there life on moss?

Tiny animals that are too small for us to see without a microscope live on moss. This plant forms a small habitat, which is a place where certain types of animals live. The moss helps the animals survive in a number of ways.

Moss

Moss provides tiny creatures with leafy food, plenty of water to drink, and leaves to hide under when predators approach.

Mossy habitat

Moss often grows in areas with lots of water—for example, around forest streams. Moss absorbs water, which makes it damp.

Nematodes

These tiny worms are found almost everywhere on the planet. They can even live in the soil beneath harsh deserts.

Bdelloid rotifers

Rotifers were around in the Earth's earliest days. They can dry themselves out and go into a kind of sleep to survive without water.

Tardigrades

These tiny animals might look cute, but they eat rotifers, nematodes, and other tardigrades! Tardigrades are normally about 0.02 in (0.5 mm) long and can live for many years without water or food.

What is the biggest living thing on the Earth?

The world's largest living thing is an 80,000-year-old grove of aspen trees in Utah. The grove shares a single root system, and each tree is genetically identical to the next.

? Quick quiz

1. What is the name of an area where an animal lives?

2. What is the Earth's biggest living thing?

3. Which tiny creature is also known as a water bear?

See pages 132–133 for the answers.

Blue planet

Much of the Earth is covered in water. Oceans, seas, lakes, and massive ice sheets all contain water. Water stored underground rises up to join rivers and can even shoot out of the ground as steam.

Why do things get carried out to sea?

Ocean water flows around the Earth in huge currents, which are like rivers. Differences in the temperature and saltiness of the water across the world, along with the pull of gravity from the moon and sun, makes the seawater move. Surface currents are driven largely by wind and can carry boats out to sea.

Windswept sea

Waves can travel around the world. They are formed by strong, persistent winds—or underwater earthquakes!

Wind currents

Wind travels in many different currents across the Earth's surface. The westerlies, the polar easterlies, and trade winds are the main wind currents that push the ocean's surface water along, creating movement.

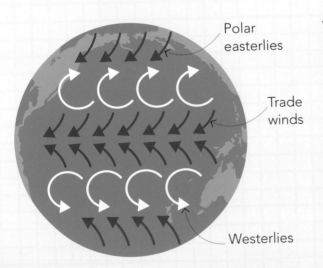

Polar easterlies

Trade winds

Westerlies

How do whirlpools form?

When opposing surface currents collide, they force each other to turn and spin. Water rushes to fill the gap, making the whirlpool bigger. The stronger the currents, the more powerful the whirlpool's spin.

Direction of current

Cold, salty currents move away from the North and South Poles. Warm currents flow away from the equator, which is the circle around the middle of the Earth.

? True or false?

1. Ocean currents are driven partly by wind.

2. Ocean currents carry warm water from the North and South Poles.

3. The westerlies are currents of water.

See pages 132–133 for the answers.

Which waves can you surf?

Ocean waves are made by energy that travels through seawater, causing the water to move. Surfers often wait for big waves that break, or fall forward, revealing a smooth wall of rising water that can carry surfers and their boards.

? True or false?

1. Waves are columns of water.

2. Spilling waves are waves that break.

3. Tsunamis are giant waves caused by earthquakes.

See pages 132–133 for the answers.

Do all waves break in the same way?

Spilling
When the tide is going out, or onshore winds blow, a gentle wave will form with foam spilling over the top.

Plunging
These waves occur when water hits an underwater obstruction or slope. The top of the wave is pushed up and tips over.

Collapsing
These are plunging waves that are not able to break in a circular motion and collapse instead.

Surging
These waves are wide and low. They move faster at the bottom than at the top.

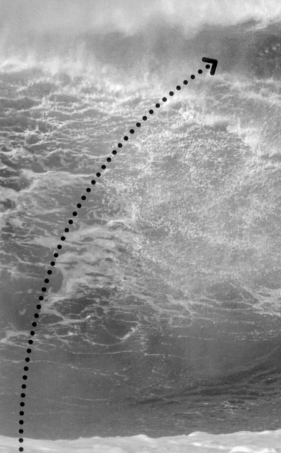

Breaking wave
Waves approaching the shore drag along the rising ocean floor. This causes the waves to tilt and collapse.

How a wave forms

Waves form as wind creates moving water. The water moves in columns of upright circles. The columns are pushed higher as the sea floor rises. The waves tilt forward to break.

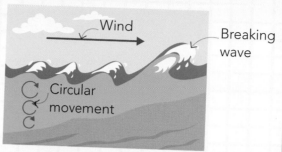

Wave formation

Wind direction

Waves travel in the direction of the wind that originally caused the water to move.

Surfing

Surfers ride the surface of breaking waves. Waves that have traveled a long way are the most powerful.

Can we drink seawater?

Seawater is plentiful—over 71 percent of all water on the Earth is in the oceans! Salt water, however, is not safe for humans to drink. It contains lots of dissolved salts, which are bad for us in large amounts. They can be removed in desalination plants to make the water drinkable.

Filtering

The water is filtered to remove small particles of sand and algae, leaving only the salty water.

Removal of debris

Seawater is sucked up from the ocean through pipes. First, any debris, such as seaweed, must be removed.

Salt water

Many salts and minerals in seawater are washed into the oceans from the land. Seawater contains lots of sodium chloride—also known as table salt.

What can live in salty oceans?

Fish
The oceans contain more than 30,000 different species of fish! They drink a lot of seawater and get rid of extra salt using their gills.

Seaweed
Plantlike seaweed, such as kelp, can hide excess salt in special parts of their cells so that it doesn't damage the rest of the seaweed.

Starfish
Starfish use seawater instead of blood. The insides of their cells are as salty as the seawater around them!

From salt to fresh
Next, the water is passed through a special membrane that allows water through but not the dissolved salts.

? Quick quiz

1. What is sodium chloride also known as?

2. Is seawater or fresh water salty?

3. Can seawater freeze?

See pages 132–133 for the answers.

Filter

Membrane

Holding tank

Drinking water
Finally, chemicals are added to clean the water and make it safe to drink. Fresh water is transported to homes, factories, or farms.

Why does the Earth need the moon?

The moon has been the Earth's companion for 4.5 billion years. It formed from the debris of a collision between the Earth during its early development and a Mars-sized planet called Theia. The Earth would be very different without the moon!

Frequent meteor strikes

The moon's gravity pulls in space debris. This protects the Earth from some meteor strikes. With no moon, the Earth would be hit by more meteors.

What else would happen without the moon?

Shorter days

The moon acts as a brake, slowing the Earth's rotation. Without the moon, the Earth would spin faster, and days might only be five hours long!

Extreme weather

The moon helps control the seasons. Without the moon, seasons could quickly change from very hot to bitterly cold.

No life

The Earth would have extreme weather and frequent meteor strikes without the moon, which might have prevented early life from developing.

How do tides happen?

As it circles the Earth, the moon's force of gravity pulls on oceans, making them bulge and swell—this is what causes tides.

The moon pulls on oceans facing it, causing high tides.

The moon also pulls the Earth toward it, so oceans on the opposite side bulge at the same time.

Brighter stars

The sun's light reflects off the moon at night, brightening up the sky and causing dim stars to fade into the background. A moonless night sky would show billions of stars.

Wildlife patterns

Some animals, such as dung beetles, use moonlight to help them navigate at night. Without it, they would be unable to find their way back home.

Much smaller tides

The moon is the main reason that tides move in and out. Without it, coastlines would be less worn away by tides.

? Quick quiz

1. How old is the moon?

2. Does the Earth's tilt change?

3. Which other body in space pulls on oceans to help cause tides?

See pages 132–133 for the answers.

Where do rivers start?

Rivers flow from water sources such as melted mountain snow, underground streams, or high-altitude lakes. From here, rivers snake their way downhill to a lake, a sea, or an ocean. Rivers can cross entire continents!

Evidence of dried-up rivers has been found on the planet Mars!

Rhine River

This is the second-largest river in Europe. It flows from the Alps through Austria, Germany, Switzerland, France, Liechtenstein, and the Netherlands.

What is the biggest river in the world?

The Amazon River in South America is the largest river on Earth. It carries almost twice as much water as the next-largest river!

Headwaters

The source of a river is called its headwaters. The point where a river reaches a lake, a sea, or an ocean is called the mouth.

Lake Toma

Lake Toma is a mountain lake in the Swiss Alps. It is thought to be the source of the Rhine River. Many lakes and streams lead to the Rhine. Lake Toma, however, is at the start of the river.

? True or false?

1. Headwaters are at the beginning of a river.

2. The Rhine is thought to begin at Lake Toma.

3. The longest river in the world is the Mississippi.

See pages 132–133 for the answers.

Can a lake be bigger than a sea?

Lake Baikal in Siberia is bigger than the state of Massachusetts and three times the size of the smallest sea, the Sea of Marmara in Turkey. Both lakes and seas are surrounded by land, but only seas are connected to oceans.

Freshwater lake

Most lakes contain fresh water. This is saltless water from inland sources such as rivers.

How are seas different from oceans?

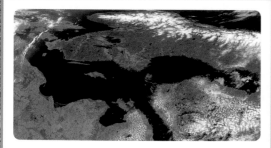

Seas are salty because they are connected to the ocean. Oceans are huge bodies of water that are not surrounded by land.

Landlocked

Most lakes, including Lake Baikal, are landlocked, or enclosed by land. • • • • • • •

Lake or sea?

Bodies of water such as the Dead Sea in the Middle East are salty but are considered lakes because they don't link to oceans. The Caspian Sea is a lake in western Asia that once connected to an ocean.

The Caspian Sea

Lake Baikal contains over 22 percent of the Earth's fresh water!

? Quick quiz

1. Is the Dead Sea a sea?

2. Do lakes connect to oceans?

3. What is the smallest sea?

See pages 132–133 for the answers.

Where is the biggest waterfall?

The biggest waterfall on Earth is under the ocean. All water on the Earth's surface flows downward because of gravity. The Denmark Strait cataract is over three times the height of the tallest waterfall above ground!

Where is it?

The Denmark Strait is a channel of the Atlantic Ocean located between Greenland and Iceland.

Warm surface water

Water near the surface of the ocean is warmed by the sun. This makes it less dense, or lighter, than colder water below.

Strong current

The rapid movement of the heavier bottom current sculpts and reshapes the Atlantic Ocean floor.

? Quick quiz

1. In which ocean is the Denmark Strait?

2. What is the tallest waterfall on land?

3. What is the tallest waterfall in the world?

See pages 132–133 for the answers.

Ocean floor

Greenland

Denmark Strait

Iceland

What are the biggest land waterfalls?

Angel Falls
This waterfall in Venezuela is the tallest on land. It falls 3,211 ft (979 m) to the valley below.

Khone Falls
The world's widest waterfall is in Laos. Khone Phapheng Falls is a staggering 35,376 ft (10,783 m) wide!

11,500 ft
(3,505 m)

Cold water overflow
An underwater river of cold water cascades over a giant underwater ridge in the Denmark Strait cataract.

Water sinks
Water cools as it flows northward near the Arctic Circle. This makes the water denser, or heavier. It sinks to the ocean floor and joins a current flowing over the cataract.

How big are icebergs?

The part of an iceberg that you can see above water is only a tiny portion of the whole thing. Icebergs are floating chunks of ice that have broken off from glaciers or huge, floating ice shelves. Icebergs can be the size of mountains!

What is the biggest body of ice on Earth?

Ice sheet

The Antarctic ice sheet is a layer of ice that covers the continent of Antarctica. It is the largest body of ice on Earth. Its ice flows into the Lambert-Fisher Glacier, a huge, slow-moving river of ice.

Floating ice

The largest floating body of ice on Earth is the Ross Ice Shelf. It is about 500 miles (800 km) wide—almost the same size as California!

Location

Most icebergs break off from Greenland's glaciers or Antarctica's ice sheets. From here, they can travel hundreds of miles.

Size

A chunk of ice has to be 16 ft (5 m) tall above sea level to be called an iceberg. Smaller ice chunks in the ocean are called bergy bits or growlers.

Underwater bulk

Around 90 percent of an iceberg is hidden below the water. This is because it is too heavy to float entirely above the surface. Ice is about 10 percent less dense than water is!

B-15 was the largest iceberg ever recorded—it was 183 miles (295 km) wide!

? Quick quiz

1. What is the biggest body of ice on the Earth?

2. How much of an iceberg is underwater?

3. What is a growler?

See pages 132–133 for the answers.

How is a glacier like a cheese grater?

Glaciers are like rivers of ice that slowly move over land. Glaciers carve out pieces of ground just as the sharp edges of a cheese grater break off bits of cheese. The biggest glaciers are found in Antarctica and Greenland.

Glacial grooves

When sharp ice or rocks in the glacier are dragged over rock and soil, it creates grooves. This is similar to how a cheese grater carves grooves into cheese!

Glacier

Glaciers are rivers of ice that form when snow builds up faster than it can melt. The snow compacts over time to form a block of ice.

Movement

Glaciers move at different speeds. This can range from 1.6 ft (0.5 m) to 98 ft (30 m) a day!

Broken rocks

Small rocks and even boulders sometimes get picked up by glaciers and carried away. These are called "erratics."

What else do melted glaciers leave behind?

Eskers

Eskers are long, winding ridges of sand and gravel left behind when glaciers melt.

Moraines

These are deposits of till, or rock and soil, that occur along the edges of a melting glacier.

Till

Glacial till is the sediment left behind when a glacier melts. It is made up of fine dust and small rocks.

? Quick quiz

1. What is an esker?

2. Do glaciers move?

3. What's the biggest glacier on the Earth?

See pages 132–133 for the answers.

What's at the bottom of the ocean?

Some parts of the ocean are less explored than nearby areas of our solar system! However, some ocean depths have been reached by robotic or crewed crafts. Here, you might find volcanoes, coral reefs, or shipwrecks.

? **Quick quiz**

1. What is an underwater mountain range called?

2. What is the name of the deepest place in the ocean?

3. Which minerals are coral skeletons made from?

See pages 132–133 for the answers.

Shipwreck

Weather, underwater hazards, or war may cause ships to sink in the ocean. Sea creatures often make their homes here.

Coral reefs

They might look like plants, but corals are actually animals! They have limestone skeletons and form communities in shallow water.

Pillow basalt

Young, pillowy basalt rocks can be found lining the ocean's floor. These are some of the newest rocks on the planet.

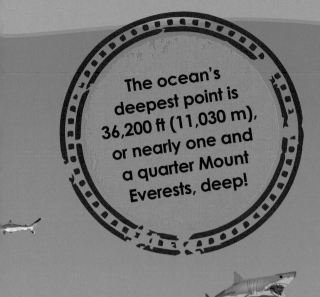

The ocean's deepest point is 36,200 ft (11,030 m), or nearly one and a quarter Mount Everests, deep!

The five oceans

One big body of water covers more than 70 percent of the Earth's surface! There are five oceans within this giant body of water: the Atlantic, Pacific, Indian, Arctic, and Southern Oceans.

Arctic Ocean

Atlantic Ocean

Pacific Ocean

Indian Ocean

Southern Ocean

Mid-ocean ridge

These are underwater mountain ranges. New ocean crust is created from molten rock that bubbles up and hardens.

Hydrothermal vents

These openings release superheated water from deep within the Earth.

Submarine cable

Long, underwater cables connect telephones and carry Wi-Fi internet between continents.

Underwater volcano

Volcanoes can form above cracks in the ocean floor. Molten rock rises and hardens in layers to form cone shapes.

Where is the ocean's twilight zone?

Below the ocean's surface are zones, or layers, of water. The deeper these get, the darker and colder they become. The twilight zone is the semidark second layer. Very different types of creatures live in each zone.

? Quick quiz

1. What is bioluminescence?

2. Which ocean zone do seahorses live in?

3. Do giant squids exist?

See pages 132–133 for the answers.

Killer whale

Sea turtle

Chain cat shark

Squid

Lantern fish

Swordfish

Seahorse

Hammerhead shark

Seal

Sunlit zone
0 to 660 ft (0 to 200 m)
Sunlight easily reaches the many creatures in this shallow zone.

Twilight zone
660 to 3,300 ft (200 to 1,000 m)
Less sunlight reaches the water in this zone. It is darker and colder than the zone above because of the lack of sunlight.

Midnight zone
3,300 to 13,100 ft (1,000 to 4,000 m)
All sunlight is absorbed by the water above, creating a dark and cold world. Some animals make their own light.

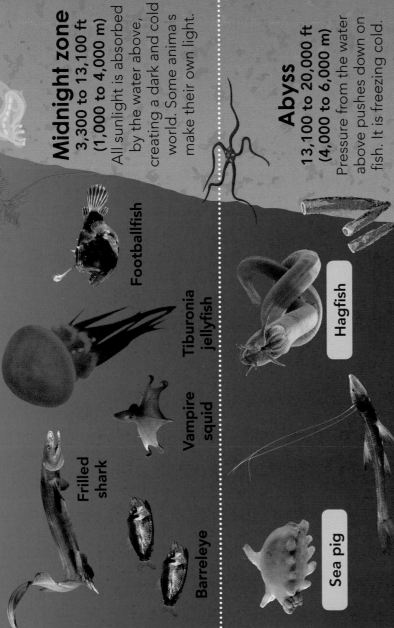

Footballfish

Tiburonia jellyfish

Vampire squid

Frilled shark

Barreleye

Abyss
13,100 to 20,000 ft (4,000 to 6,000 m)
Pressure from the water above pushes down on fish. It is freezing cold.

Hagfish

Tripod fish

Sea pig

Hadal
Below 20,000 ft (6,000 m)
Few creatures can survive here due to the total darkness and massive pressure from the water above.

Giant tube worm

Giant amphipod

How do deep-sea fish find food?

Bioluminescence
Many ocean creatures use chemicals in their bodies to create light, called bioluminescence.

Expandable stomachs
Some deep-sea fish have large jaws and stomachs that expand, allowing them to eat fish bigger than they are.

Up in the air

The weather is different around the world and changes from season to season. Rain and lightning form inside clouds that float across the sky. Powerful winds cause amazing weather spectacles, such as microbursts, hurricanes, and tornadoes.

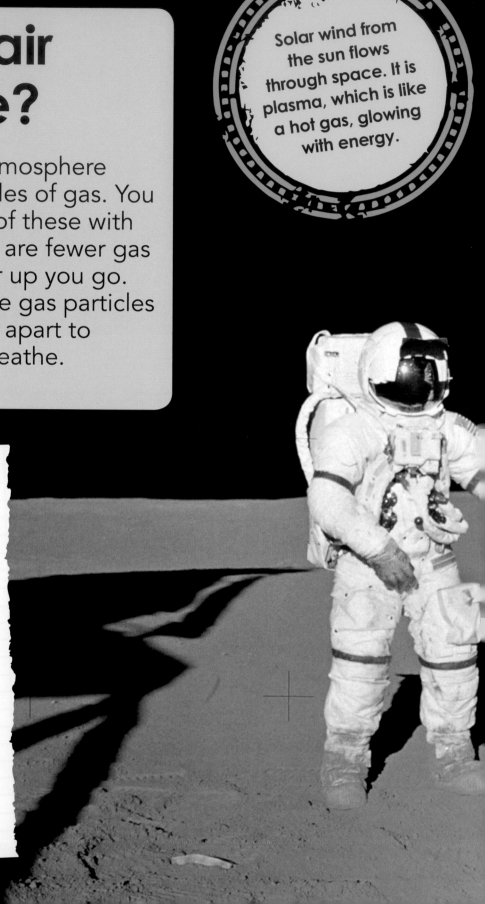

Is there air in space?

Air in the Earth's atmosphere contains tiny particles of gas. You breathe in billions of these with each breath. There are fewer gas particles the higher up you go. Space begins where gas particles are too few and far apart to make air we can breathe.

Solar wind from the sun flows through space. It is plasma, which is like a hot gas, glowing with energy.

How is air different from space?

Particles of gas are more closely packed together in air than they are in space. We breathe in a gas called oxygen to survive, which makes up around 21 percent of the air.

Air particles

Particles in space

Particles

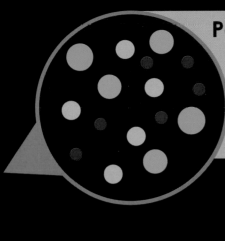

Gas particles in space are so far apart that it is nearly a vacuum, or empty space.

How does a spacecraft fly?

Modern spacecraft

Superheated gases expand from burning fuel inside modern rockets. This pushes the rocket forward.

Future rockets

Future rockets may use light itself as fuel. The light would be converted into energy to move the craft forward.

Flying the flag

It looks like there is wind blowing this flag, but the flag is actually hanging from a rod along the top! Like space, the moon has no atmosphere.

? Quick quiz

1. What is solar wind?
   a) Air blowing in space
   b) Plasma from the sun
   c) A spacecraft powered by the sun

2. Why does the flag look like it's blowing on the moon?
   a) It is blowing in the wind
   b) The astronaut is blowing it
   c) There's a secret rod along the top that holds it up

See pages 132–133 for the answers.

Why are there colors in the sky?

The sky can change color from blue to dusky red because of sunlight. Light is made up of different colors. The air breaks light up, or scatters it, into separate colors in the sky.

? Quick quiz

1. Which color is most easily scattered by the air?

2. How many colors of the rainbow are there?

3. What color are dusty skies?

See pages 132–133 for the answers.

Blue sky

A clear blue sky is the normal color of light as it enters the atmosphere. This is because blue light is most easily scattered by the air.

Yellow sky

When smoky, hazy, or dusty skies occur, light is scattered into yellowy-orange colors.

How rainbows are formed

Sunlight contains all the colors of the rainbow. When it rains, raindrops in the air bend the light. This separates the light into all of its colors.

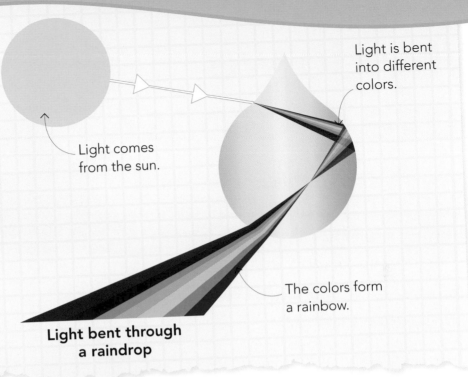

Light comes from the sun.

Light is bent into different colors.

The colors form a rainbow.

Light bent through a raindrop

Sunset

As the sun sets, its light must pass through the atmosphere sideways. Light is scattered into brilliant reds, yellows, and oranges.

Why do we have seasons?

It takes a year for the Earth to orbit (circle) the sun. During this time, the sun's energy gives us warmth and light. However, the Earth is tilted. Parts of the Earth get more or less energy depending on whether they're tilted toward or away from the sun. This creates the seasons.

New York City

Summer

During summer, your half of the Earth is tilted toward the sun. Summers are typically hot, and days are long.

? Quick quiz

1. How many days does it take the Earth to orbit the sun?

2. Do all animals hibernate?

3. Do seasons take place at the same time around the Earth?

See pages 132–133 for the answers.

Fall

This season takes place when your half of the Earth begins to tilt away from the sun. The leaves on many trees change color.

Spring

We experience spring when our half of the Earth begins to tilt toward the sun. The weather turns warmer, and plants blossom.

The Earth's axis

Winter

When the half of the Earth you live on is tilted away from the sun, winter occurs. Winters are typically cold, and the days are short.

How do seasons affect animals?

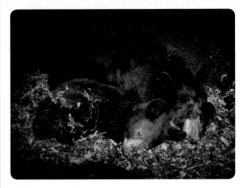

Hibernation

Many animals cannot find food during the cold winter months, so they go into a deep sleep, or hibernate, until spring comes.

Migration

Some animals just get up and move when the weather gets cold! Some birds fly to warmer places in the winter months.

Winter coats

Many animals change their bodies in winter. They get thicker, warmer coats. Arctic hares turn white to hide in snow!

Why are places hot or cold?

Sunlight does not strike the Earth evenly, so some places receive more of its heat than others. This creates hot or cold areas, called climate zones. Other things affect temperature too.

Boreal

Boreal, or taiga, climates have very long, cold winters and short, cool summers. They are typically found toward the top of the Earth, in places such as Canada or Siberia in Russia.

Tropical

The tropics are just north and south of the equator, in the equatorial zone. They are typically hot regions and can be very dry or steamy!

Hot equator

The equator is the circle around the middle of the Earth. It gets the most direct sunlight and is one of the hottest areas on our planet.

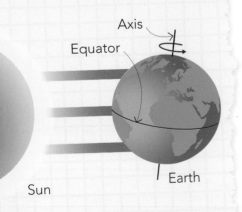

Axis

Equator

Earth

Sun

Mountain climate

High-up places such as mountains are cold. The air gets thinner and colder as you move higher up into the atmosphere.

Temperate

Areas between the tropics and the polar regions are known as temperate zones. Here, temperatures alternate between cold and warm seasons.

How does the Gulf Stream affect the climate?

This is a current of warm water in the North Atlantic Ocean. It brings warm tropical waters northward.

Mediterranean

Lands around the Mediterranean Sea have hot, dry summers and cool, often wet winters. These areas rarely get very cold because they are warmed all year round by the nearby sea.

Climate zone key

- Polar
- Boreal
- Mountain
- Temperate
- Mediterranean
- Arid
- Tropical

? Picture quiz

Why is Mount Kilimanjaro icy if it is in Tanzania, which is on the hot equator?

See pages 132–133 for the answer.

Arid

Arid, or dry, climates contain grasslands or deserts that receive very little rainfall. Deserts can be extremely hot during the day and cold at night.

Polar

These zones at the top and bottom of the Earth are the coldest places. They receive the least sunlight of any part of the planet.

Why does water fall from the sky?

The sun heats liquid water on the ground. This turns the water into a gas, which rises. High up in the sky, the gas cools down to form water droplets and ice crystals. These fall to the Earth when they become too heavy.

What is evaporation?

Liquid water becomes a gas called water vapor when it is heated or changes pressure. This process is called evaporation. In nature, the sun's heat turns the water into vapor.

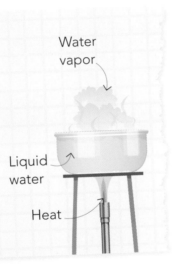

Water vapor

Liquid water

Heat

Water vapor

Liquid water becomes a gas in warm sunlight or when the air pressure decreases due to wind. Water vapor becomes part of the air.

How do people study rain and snow?

Meteorologists study the weather. They use radar to look at the liquid water and ice inside clouds, called precipitation.

Water

Rain refills liquid water sources such as rivers.

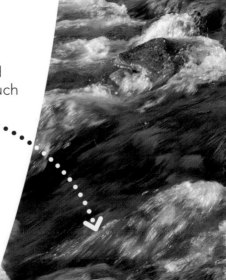

Clouds

The air gets colder higher up. Water vapor condenses, or cools down, to form water droplets. These produce clouds.

Rain

Tiny water droplets in clouds get bigger as more droplets join them. They become too heavy and fall as rain.

Mawsynram in Meghalaya State, India, is the world's wettest place. It gets around 471 in (11,971 mm) of rain every year!

? Quick quiz

1. What is the name of the process in which a liquid turns into a gas when it is heated but not boiled?

2. What is water vapor?

3. What are scientists that study the weather called?

See pages 132–133 for the answers.

How are clouds different?

Structure
Is a cloud billowy and tall, or thin and wispy? The structure, or makeup, helps us know what weather to expect.

Altitude
Wind speed, temperature, and pressure change with altitude, or height. This creates different types of cloud.

Precipitation
Water falling as snow, rain, or ice is called precipitation. Clouds that carry precipitation look different from those that don't.

Is that a dinosaur in the clouds?

Clouds form when water vapor in the sky cools and condenses, turning into ice or water droplets. These puffs of gray or white form many shapes and have different names.

Cirrus
These are the highest clouds. They are thin and wispy. Cirrus form from thin sheets of ice crystals.

Cirrocumulus
A type of cirrus cloud, these form compact patterns that are often stripy.

Altostratus
This is a thin layer of cloud in middle altitudes. It is usually a mix of liquid water and ice crystals.

36,000 ft
10,970 m

33,000 ft
10,060 m

30,000 ft
9,140 m

27,000 ft
8,230 m

24,000 ft
7,320 m

Stratocumulus

These are thick layers of mostly connected clouds. They can cause drizzly days.

Cumulus

A puffy, low cloud is called a cumulus. These rise above updrafts of hot air in the summer heat.

Dinosaur cloud

Cumulus clouds or other types can form odd shapes that inspire the imagination—such as dinosaurs.

Cumulonimbus

This is an extremely tall, sometimes scary-looking storm cloud that is usually flat at the top like an anvil.

Stratus

These low clouds form a flat-bottomed layer that may blanket the sky.

? Quick quiz

1. What are the highest clouds called?

2. What is water falling from clouds, such as rain or snow, called?

3. What is a tall, flat-topped storm cloud called?

See pages 132–133 for the answers.

21,000 ft
6,400 m

18,000 ft
5,490 m

15,000 ft
4,570 m

12,000 ft
3,660 m

9,000 ft
2,740 m

6,000 ft
1,830 m

3,000 ft
910 m

Sea level

Lightning

A lightning bolt begins when static electricity builds up in a storm cloud. The electricity starts to find its way to the ground.

Lightning rod

Metal rods on the tops of tall buildings attract lightning. A wire leads the lightning safely down to the ground.

Does lightning always strike the tallest spot?

Lightning is an electrical charge that begins in storm clouds. The tops of tall buildings can be close to the clouds, where there is lots of electricity. Lightning could hit these, but it can also strike anywhere!

Thunder clouds

Inside clouds, ice crystals and water droplets crash into each other. This creates static electricity. Lightning heats the air, expanding it and creating thunder.

Ground rod

The lightning is carried to a rod in the ground. This stops it from damaging the building.

How does lightning make rocks?

When lightning hits sand, such as on a beach, it melts the grains into glass and makes beautiful forms called fulgurites.

? True or false?

1. Lightning can strike anywhere.

2. Thunder is the sound of air that has been heated by lightning.

3. Lightning comes from static electricity.

See pages 132–133 for the answers.

Can humans make it rain?

People have tried using technology to turn water droplets and ice crystals inside clouds into rain or snow. This process is called cloud seeding. It has been used to increase snowfall in some places. However, some scientists think it does not work very well.

Aerial seeder
Aircraft carry machines that inject chemicals into clouds. These chemicals could be bad for the environment.

What is a microburst?

Microbursts are huge, natural downdrafts of wind caused by the sudden cooling of air high in the atmosphere. The rush of wind can cause damage to aircraft.

Table salt can be used to seed clouds. It causes water droplets to join together as raindrops.

Clouds

Clouds that contain lots of water droplets and ice crystals are often the targets of seeding.

Seeding

Different chemicals are used. Some attract water droplets, which join together to form rain. Others attract ice crystals to form large snowflakes.

? Quick quiz

1. Which household substance can be used to seed clouds?

2. Can we make it rain without clouds?

3. What joins together to form rain?

See pages 132–133 for the answers.

How does a tornado form?

Tornadoes are rotating columns of air that can spin at speeds of over 300 mph (482 kph)! The air beneath some storms begins to rise and spin, forming a mesocyclone. If a downward flow of air forms next to the mesocyclone, a tornado can develop.

Tornado

A downward draft of air can form next to the rising air. Tornadoes often occur when this happens.

How do we measure the strength of tornadoes?

In the United States, tornadoes are ranked from zero to five on the Enhanced Fujita (EF) scale.

EF-0 tornado

An EF-0 tornado is the weakest, causing minimal damage. It has the lowest wind speeds of any tornado.

EF-5 tornado

These tornadoes are the most powerful. EF-5s can be a mile (1.6 km) wide and destroy most things in their path.

Spinning air

Tornadoes form beneath parent storm clouds. Rising air starts to spin high above the ground.

Dusty base

The tornado pulls in dust, debris, and other objects in its path. This gives it a brown or gray color.

What is a hurricane?

Also called tropical cyclones, hurricanes are spinning storm clouds that form over some parts of the ocean. Hurricanes that reach land can cause a huge amount of damage.

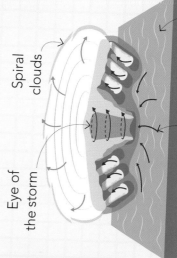

Eye of the storm

Spiral clouds

Surface winds

Ocean

? Quick quiz

1. Which scale measures the strength of tornadoes?

2. What type of storm cloud might tornadoes form beneath?

3. What is the center of a hurricane called?

See pages 132–133 for the answers.

Living on the Earth

The number of humans on the Earth has continued to grow throughout history. Our planet provides water, food, air to breathe, and fuel to create energy. We have changed the Earth in many ways and need to make sure we take care of it.

How many people live on the Earth?

At the last count, there were more than 7.8 billion people on the Earth. If we all stood next to each other in a line, it would stretch around the world more than 88 times! We need to make sure there are enough resources, such as food and water, for everyone.

Which natural resources are essential for human survival?

Food
Most food is grown on farms and transported to stores. Scientists are researching other ways to get food in case we run out of space to farm.

Water
Clean water is hard to get in areas where there aren't lakes or rivers. Water can't be made, so we have to share what's there.

Overpopulation
The population of the Earth is growing. There are only enough natural resources for about 10 billion people.

Tokyo

Japan's capital, Tokyo, is one of the world's largest cities. There are almost 16,000 people per square mile.

World population

Every country in the world has a different-sized population. Some populations are growing at a fast rate. Others, such as Japan, are actually shrinking.

World population by continent

Key

Most populated — Least populated

? Quick quiz

1. How many people can the world's natural resources support?

2. Is the world's population growing?

3. What is the capital of Japan?

See pages 132–133 for the answers.

How do countries begin?

For hundreds of thousands of years, humans have lived in tribes. Over time, these groups grew and combined. People moved to new areas and developed their own cultures and governments, eventually forming countries.

Colonization

Throughout history, people have traveled to new lands and claimed them as their own, even if people were already living there. British settlers colonized parts of North America, which later became the USA.

Settlers sailing to North America

Military parade, Colombia

USA

Colombia

? Quick quiz

1. What is the oldest country that exists today?

2. Which mountain range separates France and Spain?

3. Which country was built from a farming community along the River Nile?

See pages 132–133 for the answers.

Independence

Sometimes, colonies rebel against the ruling country in order to become independent, or govern themselves. Colombia became independent from Spain in 1819.

Joining together

Some nations join together to form one larger country. Together, England, Scotland, Wales, and Northern Ireland make up the UK.

What makes a country unique?

Languages

Languages allow people to communicate. They may change over time as new words are invented.

Religion

Religions provide a set of beliefs around which people gather together. Countries may have one main religion, or many.

Culture

Culture is the shared traditions and customs, such as food, dress, and art, of a society, place, or group of people that develop over time.

UK

France

Spain

Egypt

Pyrenees, France

Natural boundaries

Landforms, such as mountain ranges, deserts, rivers, and oceans, can form barriers that separate distinct cultures. Many of these features create borders between countries.

Australia

Island countries

Islands are often isolated and develop into single countries with the ocean surrounding them. Australia is an "island" country.

Farms along the Nile, Egypt

Farming together

Early people lived together in settlements to produce food. Farming meant people could stay in one place rather than moving around to hunt. These settlements eventually became countries.

How have we changed the Earth?

Humans live on every continent and have changed the surface of the Earth forever. We use many natural resources, shape the land, and build huge cities.

? Picture quiz

What is this ancient creature that was hunted to extinction by humans?

See pages 132–133 for the answer.

Dammed lake

The O'Shaughnessy Dam in California created the Hetch Hetchy reservoir. It flooded a whole valley with water.

River valley

Damming a river changes the landscape dramatically. The lake created behind a dam floods the ground and covers trees.

Before

After

How else have we affected the Earth?

Farming

We have built farms over large areas of the Earth's surface to raise animals and grow crops, such as rice. Forests are often cleared to make space for farms, and rivers are diverted to water crops.

Deforestation

Forests are cut down to clear land for farms and cities and to produce wood for building or fuel. Without trees, soil can wash away, and the land can become a desert.

Over 83 percent of land on the Earth has been changed by humans.

Modern city

Cities can be huge and produce lots of waste. Tall skyscrapers change the skyline, like those in Panama City, Panama.

Growing town

Even small towns change the land around them. Farms are built to grow food, the course of rivers can be changed to provide water, and forests are cut down to make space for houses.

Before

After

What is a city?

Cities are places where large groups of people live close together. In cities, people often have access to useful services such as hospitals, schools, and stores.

Education

City governments are often in charge of schools. Universities provide education for older students.

Religion

Places where people can practice religion, such as cathedrals, have always been a major part of city life.

Stores

Cities may have first started so that people could trade, or exchange, goods. Modern cities have stores that sell goods.

Berlin, Germany

How tall can a building be?

The Jeddah Tower is currently being built in Saudi Arabia. It could be the tallest building ever, at over 0.6 miles (1 km) high.

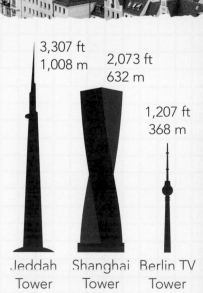

3,307 ft
1,008 m

2,073 ft
632 m

1,207 ft
368 m

Jeddah Tower

Shanghai Tower

Berlin TV Tower

Health and safety

City hospitals help provide health care for people. Ambulances zoom through the air and on the ground to take people to the hospital.

Berlin TV Tower

Public transport

Different forms of transportation, such as buses, rental bikes, subways, and streetcars, allow many people to travel quickly around a city.

Government

Cities are managed by governments. Their job can include keeping people safe by enforcing laws to stop bad behavior.

Have there always been cities?

Cities may date back as far as 10,000 years ago. Cities grew from towns, which were likely begun so that groups of people could better protect themselves and trade goods with others.

? Picture quiz

According to legend, which twins built the city of Rome in Italy?

See pages 132–133 for the answer.

How do we feed everyone?

Keeping the billions of people on the Earth alive requires a lot of food! Many groups of people rely on wheat to make bread and pasta. Wheat is grown in places with the right climate and soil and then sent around the world.

Wheat

Wheat grains are separated from the stalks. The grain is stored in tall buildings called silos to protect it from insects and rain.

Staple crops

Wheat, corn, soybeans, and rice are staple crops available around the world. These are grown in places with the right soils and climates.

Corn

Soy bean

Rice

Combine harvester

Machines help us produce lots of food. Combines are used to collect much more wheat than people can gather by hand.

? Quick quiz

1. Which crop is usually used to make bread?

2. Which machine is often used to gather wheat?

3. What is the farming of animals also known as?

See pages 132–133 for the answers.

China, India, Russia, and the United States are the largest producers of food crops in the world.

Wheat field

Vast fields of wheat can be seen in Kansas. Around the world, wheat is used to make flour for pasta, bread, and cakes.

How else do we get food?

Fishing

Fishing is a major source of food for regions bordering bodies of water. Fish, shrimp, and other marine life are often farmed in oceans, lakes, and rivers.

Animal farming

Animal husbandry is the farming of animals for food. Cows, pigs, chickens, and other animals are raised for their meat.

Gathering

Early humans gathered nuts, berries, and fruit in the wild. The finding and gathering of these foods still occurs today.

How do we find our way around?

To find our way around a new place, we need to know where we are and where everything else is. Maps describe the area around us. The pictures match up with real-life features that we can spot as we explore.

Rivers

Blue lines show rivers and waterways. If you need to get somewhere by a blue line, look out for a river!

Compass bearings

A compass shows the direction you're going in, be it north, east, south, or west. The arrow points toward the Earth's magnetic North Pole.

Roads

White or black lines on a map usually show roads. The thicker the line, the bigger the road.

Grid references

A grid is often drawn on maps to help the reader find a place. The horizontal lines are numbered and the vertical lines are lettered. Together, these provide a grid reference for each square—for example, "C1".

Colors

Different colors on a map often match the features they're showing. If you're by a grassy area, look for green!

What are longitude and latitude?

Equator

Meridian line

Latitude is your distance north or south of the Earth's equator. Longitude is how far you are east or west of Europe's meridian line.

Symbols

Pictures, or symbols, are used to show important features. A train station might be indicated by a train symbol, for example.

True or false?

1. The prime meridian line runs through Europe.

2. North is the direction toward the bottom of the Earth.

3. On a map, roads are shown by blue lines.

See pages 132–133 for the answers.

Landmarks

Areas have unique places, or landmarks. Maps often show these so that you can find them easily.

Some scientists think that, by weight, there will be more plastic than fish in the oceans by 2050!

Loose litter
Rainwater can carry plastic from trash cans or other garbage sites into rivers, which lead into the ocean.

Plastic pollution
Plastic is used to make everything from airplane parts to food packaging. Lots of this ends up in oceans.

How much plastic is in the ocean?

Millions of tons of plastic makes its way into our oceans each year. Lots of this comes from food or beverage packaging. We can help reduce the amount of plastic in oceans by using fewer plastic items or by recycling the ones we do use.

Microplastics

Plastics in the ocean eventually break down into smaller pieces. Seawater contains billions of these tiny bits of plastic.

Why is plastic bad for oceans?

Harmful to wildlife

Wildlife can get tangled up in plastic. This makes it hard for the animal to find food or escape predators.

Plastic food

Sea life can accidentally eat tiny bits of ocean plastic, called microplastics. Plastic found in sea life could be harmful to humans who eat it.

Great Pacific garbage patch

A huge patch of plastic can be found in the Pacific Ocean. It is around three times the size of France and contains about 88,185 tons of floating waste!

Garbage is pulled into large patches by rotating currents, called gyres.

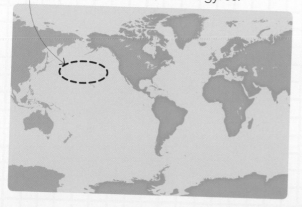

? Quick quiz

1. How much does the plastic in the Great Pacific Garbage Patch weigh?

2. What are rotating ocean currents called?

See pages 132–133 for the answers.

What is recycling?

If you recycle something, it gets turned into a new object. Many of the natural materials we use to make things will one day run out. Recycling human-made items means they don't go to waste. Here's how it works.

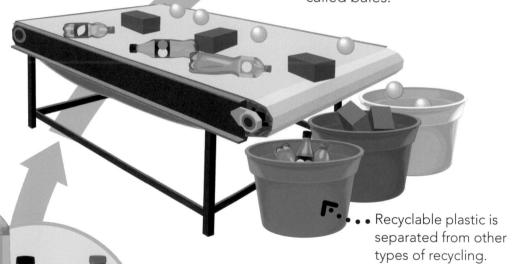

Bales

The plastic is crushed and made into blocks called bales.

Sorting

Materials that can be recycled first need to be sorted by type. Plastic, glass, and cardboard are all recycled separately.

Recyclable plastic is separated from other types of recycling.

Some, but not all, plastics can be recycled.

Plastic pellets

PET pellets can be melted down and poured into molds to make new objects, such as bottles.

Plastic bottles

A material called polyethylene terephthalate, or PET, is found in most plastic bottles. This can be used to make new plastic objects.

Flakes

The bales are chopped up into small flakes of plastic.

The melted PET hardens into a lump and is cut into pellets.

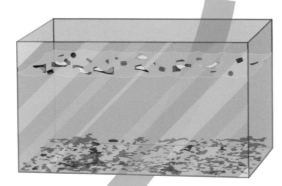

Cleaning

Water separates the PET from the parts of the bottle that can't be recycled. The heavy PET sinks. Labels and other materials that can't be recycled float upward.

Melting and chopping

The PET flakes are melted. The liquid plastic hardens into a lump. The lump is chopped into pellets.

? True or false?

1. All materials can be recycled.

2. Materials that can be recycled need to be recycled by type.

3. PET is a recyclable material found in plastic.

See pages 132–133 for the answers.

What else can be recycled?

Paper

Paper trash is mashed up, mixed with water, and heated. This mixture is strained and rolled out into new paper.

Metal

Metal that can be recycled is cleaned and heated until it melts. The liquid metal is then poured into bar-shaped molds. The metal cools and hardens into bars that can be shaped into new objects.

How bad is a drought?

We call a long, rainless period a drought. When a drought occurs, it can cause problems for both plants and animals. Droughts usually happen in dry areas and can last for many years.

Wildfire

Dry winds fuel wildfires. These spread quickly through dried-out trees in forests.

It didn't rain for 14 years in Arica, Chile, between 1903 and 1918!

Dust storm

Rain keeps soil stuck together and stops it from blowing away. Without rain, soil loosens into dust and is blown into huge clouds by the wind.

Parched land

Without moisture from rain, soils crack and harden in the sun. The land becomes a dry, almost lifeless desert.

Crop failure

Crops need water to survive. In a drought, water sources can run out because they aren't being replenished. This means farmers can't keep their crops alive.

Dust devil

These minicyclones often form in sunny conditions when there is very little wind. Heated by the sun, air rises quickly, pulling in dirt and dust. This creates dust devils that roam the countryside.

How can we save water during a drought?

Take shorter showers
The average shower uses the equivalent of 270 glasses of water!

Farm fewer animals
Cows drink up to 20 times the amount of water that humans do. If we raised fewer cows for meat, we'd save a lot of water.

Is the Earth getting warmer?

The Earth's climate changes naturally over time. It has been both warmer and colder in the past. We live in a relatively cool period today, but human activity is causing temperatures to rise more quickly than ever before.

20,000 years ago

Around 2.6 million years ago, the Earth began to cool. The ice that covered a lot of the planet only began to melt 20,000 years ago.

120 years ago

The growth of factories increased the amount of greenhouse gases being released into the air, further warming the planet.

56 million years ago

The Earth was quite hot in the past! About 56 million years ago, the Earth was so warm, there was no ice at the North Pole!

12.6°F (7°C)
warmer than now

9°F (5°C)
colder than now

1.8°F (1°C)
colder than now

Present day

The Earth is getting warmer faster than ever. Greenhouse gases from vehicles and power plants speed up natural warming. Awareness is helping bring about cleaner air.

Greenhouse gases

The atmosphere acts like a greenhouse. The sun warms the Earth, and the atmosphere traps some of the heat. Certain gases, called greenhouse gases, trap extra heat.

Greenhouse gases in the air trap more heat.

The atmosphere traps the heat.

The sun heats the Earth.

Picture quiz

Which planet has a thick atmosphere of greenhouse gases?

See pages 132–133 for the answer.

80 years in the future

The Earth may become warmer than today. Areas of ice may have melted into the oceans. This extra water could flood coastal areas.

Current temperature

5.4°F (3°C) warmer than now

Oxygen

Humans need to breathe in a gas called oxygen to survive. Trees release oxygen into the air.

Carbon dioxide

Trees take a gas called carbon dioxide out of the air. This gas traps heat in the atmosphere. Too much of it can make the Earth hotter.

How do trees help humans?

Trees help create the oxygen that we need in order to survive. Their roots take in water from the ground, which stops flooding. They can even increase the amount of rain in an area because the water evaporates from their leaves.

? Quick quiz

1. What gas do trees release into the air?

2. What is the name of the process in which plants make glucose?

See pages 132–133 for the answers.

How can eating insects save trees?

Forests are chopped down to make way for farmland. This is used to raise animals for meat. Some people choose to eat foods that aren't produced using lots of land, such as insects.

Photosynthesis

Plants make their own food through a process called photosynthesis. They use sunlight, carbon dioxide, and water to make a type of sugar called glucose. Oxygen is also made and released into the air.

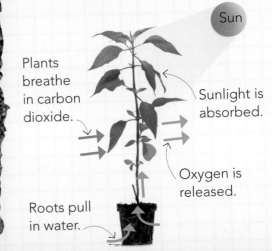

Sun

Plants breathe in carbon dioxide.

Sunlight is absorbed.

Oxygen is released.

Roots pull in water.

The human effect

When we burn fuel in cars or to power electricity plants, it produces carbon dioxide.

What is the future of energy?

Power plants that create electricity have mainly burned fossil fuels up to this time. Supplies of these fuels, such as crude oil, will become harder to find. Carbon dioxide is produced when fossil fuels burn, making the Earth warmer. People are slowly switching to different, less damaging, ways to make electricity.

Every 10 seconds, enough crude oil to fill an Olympic swimming pool is taken out of the ground.

Wind energy

Large windmills contain turbines used to create electricity. Most turbines are on land, but they can also be built in the ocean.

Tidal energy

The movement of oceans in tides can be used to generate, or make, energy.

Water

Water on the Earth flows downhill. Hydroelectric power plants use this movement to create electricity.

Solar energy

Light from the sun provides solar energy. Solar panels can be installed almost anywhere but only generate power during the daytime.

How can we use less energy?

Riding a bike

Riding a bike uses only human energy, so it saves the Earth's natural energy resources. It is cleaner for the environment and healthier for you!

Saving energy

Using less energy helps us stretch our energy sources further and makes them last longer. Turning off the lights helps us be good caretakers of our planet!

Nuclear energy

Huge amounts of energy come from splitting apart tiny particles. The radioactive materials used in nuclear plants must be stored safely.

Biofuel

Biofuels come from plants such as corn and sugarcane. These can be burned like fossil fuels in power plants or vehicles.

? Quick quiz

1. What is plant fuel called?

2. What kind of energy does the sun provide?

3. Which type of power plant uses radioactive material?

See pages 132–133 for the answers.

Answers

Page 9 1) The sun came first. 2) Around 4.6 billion years ago. 3) The Earth is a rocky planet.

Page 11 Aurora.

Page 12 1) A meteor that has fallen to the Earth. 2) No. The Earth moves around the sun.

Page 15 1) Yes. It is solid iron and nickel. 2) Two thirds. The remaining one third is continental crust. 3) No. The crust is broken into segments, or plates.

Page 17 1) True. 2) True. 3) False. There is some gravity from bodies in space.

Page 19 Jupiter.

Page 21 1) Around 4 billion years old. 2) Yes. Crocodiles are related to dinosaurs. 3) 65 million years ago.

Page 23 A hippo.

Page 25 1) Over 2.17 miles (3.5 km) thick. 2) Around 10,000 BCE. 3) Yes. The location of New York City was under ice during the last ice age.

Page 28 1) False. It formed from lava produced by volcanoes. 2) True. 3) False. The Isua Greenstone Belt of Greenland, is believed to be the oldest.

Page 31 1) True. 2) False. It becomes rock when it cools and hardens.

Page 33 1) Volcanic ash or mud. 2) Yellowstone National Park. 3) 380 ft (116 m).

Page 34 1) False. Humus is the top layer. 2) True. 3) True.

Page 37 1) True. 2) True. 3) False. Minerals are natural solids.

Page 39 1) b. 2) a.

Page 41 1) About 10,000–14,000 years ago. 2) Weathering. 3) Yes.

Page 43 1) Mineral deposits. 2) The Colorado River. 3) Sandstone.

Page 45 1) True. 2) False. They record movements of living things. 3) True.

Page 47 1) False. It is in Antarctica. 2) False. Some deserts are very cold at night.

Page 49 1) The surface of Thailand is made up of many caves and sinkholes.

Page 51 1) A stalagmite grows from the floor. 2) No. It is mildly acidic and only wears away rocks. 3) A column.

Page 53 1) Molten rock rises up through seafloor cracks and hardens. 2) The Anatolian plate. 3) Around 90 percent.

Page 55 1) True. 2) True.

Page 57 1) Farmland. 2) Desert. 3) The Amazon Rainforest.

Page 59 1) False. It is a type of salamander. 2) False. A manatee is also known as a sea cow. 3) False. They are different species.

Page 61 1) A habitat. 2) A grove of Aspen trees in Utah. 3) A tardigrade.

Page 65 1) True. 2) False. Cold water is carried from the North and South Poles. 3) False. They are wind currents.

Page 66 1) True. 2) True. 3) True.

Page 69 1) The mineral halite or salt. 2) Seawater. 3) Yes. Seawater freezes at a lower temperature than fresh water.

Page 71 1) Around 4.5 billion years old. 2) Yes. The Earth wobbles over long periods of time—about every 26,000 years! 3) The sun.

Page 73 1) True. 2) True. 3) False. It is the Amazon River in South America.

Page 75 1) No. It is a lake. 2) No. Seas do. 3) The Sea of Marmara is the world's smallest.

Page 76 1) The Atlantic Ocean. 2) Angel Falls. 3) The Denmark Strait cataract.

Page 79 1) The Antarctic ice sheet. 2) Around 90 percent. 3) A chunk of ice in the ocean that is smaller than an iceberg or a bergy bit.

Page 81 1) A long, winding ridge of sediment left by a glacier. 2) Yes. Glaciers move like rivers of ice. 3) The Lambert-Fisher Glacier in Antarctica.

Page 82 1) A mid-ocean ridge. 2) Challenger Deep in the Mariana Trench. 3) Calcite and aragonite, which make up the rock limestone.

Page 84 1) Light created by animals using chemicals. 2) The sunlit zone. 3) Yes. Giant squids exist.

Page 89 1) b. 2) c.

Page 90 1) Blue light. 2) Seven main colors blend to form millions of shades. 3) Yellow.

Page 92 1) 365 days. 2) No. Only some animals who live in places with very cold winters hibernate. 3) No. Different places are tilted toward or away from the sun depending on the time of year. This means they have different seasons.

Page 95 Mount Kilimanjaro is a mountain with a mountain climate, which means it gets cold even though it is near the equator.

Page 97 1) Evaporation. 2) Water vapor is the gas version of water. 3) Meteorologists.

Page 99 1) Cirrus clouds. 2) Precipitation. 3) A cumulonimbus cloud.

Page 101 1) True. It only sometimes strikes the tallest spot. 2) True. 3) True.

Page 103 1) Table salt. 2) No. Cloud seeding uses clouds to try to make rain fall. 3) Water droplets.

Page 105 1) The Enhanced Fujita (EF) scale. 2) A cumulonimbus cloud. 3) The eye of the storm.

Page 109 1) Around 10 billion. 2) Yes. The population is growing. 3) Tokyo.

Page 110 1) China. 2) The Pyrenees. 3) USA.

Page 112 The woolly mammoth.

Page 115 Romulus and Remus.

Page 117 1) Wheat. 2) A combine harvester. 3) Animal husbandry.

Page 119 1) True. 2) False. North is the direction toward the top of the Earth. South is downward. 3) False. They are shown by black or white lines.

Page 121 1) About 88,185 tons (80,000 tonnes). 2) Gyres.

Page 123 1) False. Only certain types of material can be recycled. 2) True. 3) True.

Page 125 1) c. 2) b.

Page 127 Venus.

Page 129 1) Oxygen. 2) Photosynthesis.

Page 131 1) Biofuel. 2) Solar energy. 3) A nuclear power plant.

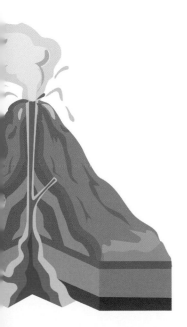

Quiz your friends!

Who knows the most about the Earth? Test your friends and family with these tricky questions. See pages 136–137 for the answers.

Questions

1. What is the name of the **supercontinent** that existed around **330 million years** ago?

5. What is fossilized poop called?

9. How much **warmer** was the Earth **56 million years** ago?

10. What type of rock is made by lightning?

2. What is the **imaginary circle** around the **middle** of the Earth called?

4. What is the **deepest** ocean zone?

3. How long would a day on the Earth be without the moon?

8. Which place holds the **record** for the **hottest temperature** on the Earth?

6. What are **low, fluffy clouds** called?

7. Which term refers to large areas of **forestland** being **cut down**?

11. What is the name of the line where **space begins**?

12. What is the **largest desert** in the world?

13. What are **tiny bits** of broken-down **plastic** called?

14. What is the name of the landform that shoots out hot water?

15. How much of an iceberg is **underwater**?

Answers

1. Pangaea

8. The **hottest** temperatur
on record was at **Death
Valley, USA.**

13. **Microplastics**

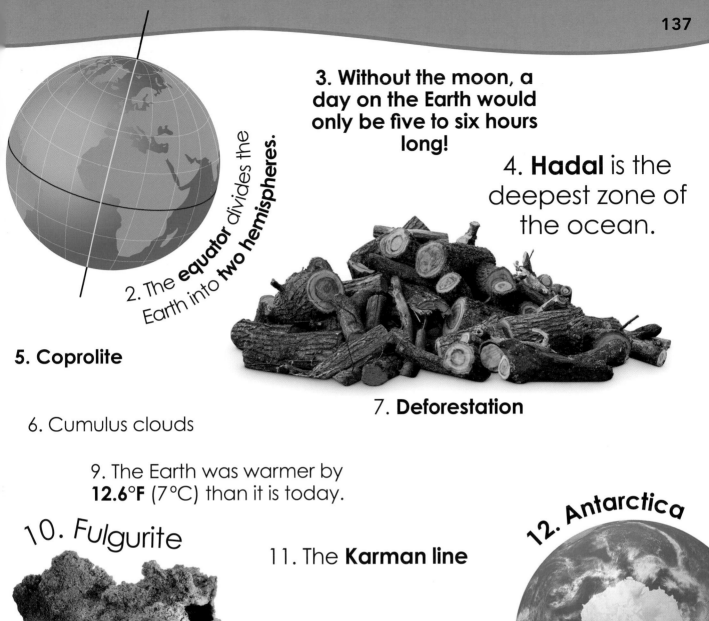

3. Without the moon, a day on the Earth would only be five to six hours long!

4. Hadal is the deepest zone of the ocean.

2. The **equator** divides the Earth into **two hemispheres.**

5. Coprolite

6. Cumulus clouds

7. Deforestation

9. The Earth was warmer by **12.6°F** (7°C) than it is today.

10. *Fulgurite*

11. The **Karman line**

12. Antarctica

14. Geysers shoot out hot water and steam.

15. **90 percent** of an iceberg is underwater.

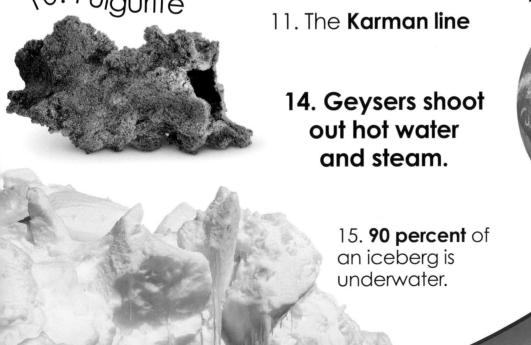

Glossary

acidic
Containing a chemical that can wear away certain materials

adaptation
When a species develops features to help it survive in a certain area

air
Gases that form the Earth's atmosphere

artificial
Made by humans

ash
Small bits of rock that erupt out of volcanoes

atmosphere
Layer of gases surrounding the Earth

atoms
Tiny particles that make up gases, liquids, and solids

axis
Invisible line through the center of the Earth, around which the planet rotates

bacteria
Small living things that can usually be seen only with a microscope

bedrock
Layer of rock beneath the ground

biome
Area where living things share common features that help them survive in their climate

boreal forest
Cold biome with freezing temperatures for around half the year, also known as taiga

carbon dioxide
Gas found in the atmosphere that makes the Earth warmer

climate
Usual temperature and amount of precipitation in a specific area

cloud
Floating mass of water droplets or ice crystals

continent
Huge area of land, usually made up of different countries

core
Extremely hot center of the Earth

crust
Outer rocky layer of the Earth

current
Flow of water, air, or electricity

desert
Area that receives very little precipitation, such as rain or snow

earthquake
Shaking of the Earth due to the activity of plates beneath the surface

ecosystem
Community of living things in an area

energy
Force that causes things to happen, such as movement

equator
Imaginary circle around the middle of the Earth

erosion
Movement of rock by wind, rain, or ice from one place to another

evaporation
Process of liquid water being heated to become a gas

extinction
When a species dies out completely

fossil
Remains of a plant or an animal or its activities preserved in stone

gemstone
Beautiful or valuable type of mineral

glacier
Large body of ice that slowly moves across land like a river

government
Group of people that run a country, city, etc.

gravity
Force that pulls things together

habitat
Area where a type of animal usually lives

Karman line
Imaginary line marking the place where the Earth's atmosphere ends and space begins

landform
Natural, rocky feature found on land or at the bottom of the ocean

lava
Molten rock that has erupted above the ground

lightning
Electrical charge that forms in clouds, caused by ice crystals and water droplets crashing into each other

magma
Molten rock beneath the ground

Mediterranean
Area around the Mediterranean Sea with typically hot summers and cool winters

mineral
Natural solids made up of crystal shapes

molten
Something that has been melted into a liquid

moon
Natural body that orbits the Earth

ocean
Large body of water that is not enclosed by land

orbit
Circular path of an object being pulled around another body by gravity

oxygen
Gas in the atmosphere that both land animals and fish breathe

petroleum
Natural liquid made from the remains of buried plants and animals

planet
Huge, spherical object found naturally in space

plastic
Artificial material used to make many items, which does not break down easily

plate
Large segment of rock beneath the Earth's surface, forming part of the Earth's crust

polar
Icy area that is near the North or South Pole and is cold all year round

poles
Imaginary points at the top and bottom of the Earth

population
Number of people in an area

precipitation
Water that falls from clouds as liquid or ice

pressure
Force of something pressing on another object

season
Period of similar weather at a certain time of the year

sediment
Small pieces of rock, such as sand

solar
Relating to the sun

solar system
The sun and bodies that orbit it

species
Type of animal or plant

star
Huge body of burning gas in space

temperate
Mild climate zone that usually has warm summers and cool winters

thunder
Sound made by air expanding in clouds because it has been heated by lightning

tides
Movement of oceans caused by the pull of gravity from the moon and the sun

tornado
Column of spinning wind extending from storm clouds down to the ground

tropical
Warm climate zone close to the equator

volcano
Crack in the Earth's surface through which molten rock erupts

weathering
When small pieces of rock are broken off larger rocks by wind, rain, or water

Index

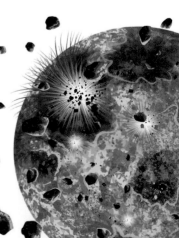

Acknowledgments

DORLING KINDERSLEY would like to thank: Ann Cannings for jacket design; Abhijeet Dutta and Ishani Nandi for editorial; Caroline Hunt for proofreading; and Helen Peters for the index.

Smithsonian Enterprises
Kealy Gordon **Product Development Manager**
Jill Corcoran **Director, Licensed Publishing**
Brigid Ferraro **Vice President, Business Development and Licensing**
Carol LeBlanc **President**

The publisher would like to thank the following for their kind permission to reproduce their photographs:

(Key: a-above; b-below/bottom; c-centre; f-far; l-left; r-right; t-top)

1 123RF.com: Wilfred Marissen (br); tebnad (fbl/Wind Turbine); Dr Ajay Kumar Singh (crb/Sunflowers). **Dorling Kindersley:** 01253854 (clb); Suhas Asnikar / Mangala Purushottam (clb/Bonsai, br/Bonsai); The Natural History Museum, London (crb/Butterflies). **Dreamstime.com:** Adambowers (cb); Cyberfyber (fbl, clb/Buildings, crb/Buildings); Igor Dymov (clb/Copenhagen); Sergey Uryadnikov / Surz01 (clb/Kelp Gull); Deymos (crb/Building); Tetiana Zbrodko / Ta (bl, crb/Chrysanthemum); Demerzel21 (br/Tower). **NASA:** NOAA / GSFC / Suomi NPP / VIIRS / Norman Kuring (bc/Earth). **2 Dorling Kindersley:** The Natural History Museum, London (bl, bc). **3 123RF.com:** Wilfred Marissen (crb/Spoonbill); tebnad (clb/Wind Turbine); Dr Ajay Kumar Singh (bc/Sunflowers, crb/Sunflowers). **Alamy Stock Photo:** Simon Belcher (br). **Dorling Kindersley:** 01253854 (cb/Frog); The Natural History Museum, London (cb/Butterflies); Suhas Asnikar / Mangala Purushottam (cb/Bonsai, crb); Twan Leenders (bc/Snake). **Dreamstime.com:** Adambowers (cb/Krakatoa); Sergey Uryadnikov / Surz01 (cb); Deymos (cb/Building); Igor Dymov (cb/Copenhagen); Cyberfyber (cb/Buildings, cb/Buildings Left, clb/Buildings, bc/Buildings); Tetiana Zbrodko / Ta (cb/Chrysanthemum, crb/Chrysanthemum); Steve Byland / Stevebyland (bc); Ongchangwei (bc/Mountain); Demerzel21 (bc/Tower). **NASA:** NOAA / GSFC / Suomi NPP / VIIRS / Norman Kuring (bc/Earth). **4 Dorling Kindersley:** Simon Mumford / NASA (cra). **5 123RF.com:** Irina Pommer (tr). **Alamy Stock Photo:** World History Archive (c). **Science Photo Library:** Eye Of Science (bl). **6 123RF.com:** Dr Ajay Kumar Singh (cra/Sunflowers); tebnad (tl/Wind Turbine, cla/Wind Turbine). **Dorling Kindersley:** Twan Leenders (cra/Snake); Suhas Asnikar / Mangala Purushottam (tl/Bonsai, tr/Bonsai). **Dreamstime.com:** Cyberfyber (tl/Buildings, cla/Buildings, cr/Buildings); Steve Byland / Stevebyland (fcl); Ongchangwei (cra/Mountain); Demerzel21 (cra/Tower); Tetiana Zbrodko / Ta (cla/Chrysanthemum, tr/Chrysanthemum). **NASA:** NOAA / GSFC / Suomi NPP / VIIRS / Norman Kuring (t/Earth). **6-7 123RF.com:** Russ McElroy / russ9358 (b). **7 123RF.com:** Wilfred Marissen (tl/Spoonbill). **8-9 ESA:** NASA (Background). **10-11 Dreamstime.com:** Serge Bogomyako / Sergebogomyako (c). **10 NASA:** (bc). **U.S. Air Force:** (c). **11 123RF.com:** filmfoto (cb); Russ McElroy / russ9358 (cr). **Dreamstime.com:** Lars Christensen / C-foto (c); Ulkass (cb/Clouds). **12 Dreamstime.com:** Andras Csontos (cra). **12-13 Dorling Kindersley:** NASA (c/main). **13 Getty Images:** Barcroft (bl). **16 Dreamstime.com:** Andrey Armyagov (bl); Andygaylor (cl). **ESA:** Herschel / PACS / MESS Key Programme Supernova Remnant Team; NASA, ESA and Allison Loll / Jeff Hester (Arizona State University) (bc). **16-17 123RF.com:** swavo (Background). **17 Dreamstime.com:** Dio5050 (cl); Alexander Pladdet / Pincarel (c). **Fotolia:** robynmac (cb/Ball). **18 123RF.com:** tebnad (cr). **Dorling Kindersley:** Suhas Asnikar / Mangala Purushottam (cra/Bonsai). **Dreamstime.com:** Cyberfyber (cra, crb/Buildings); Tetiana Zbrodko / Ta (crb/Chrysanthemum); Steve Byland / Stevebyland (crb/Hummingbird). **NASA:** JPL (crb/Venus). **18-19 NASA:** NOAA / GSFC / Suomi NPP / VIIRS / Norman Kuring (c/Earth). **19 123RF.com:** Wilfred Marissen (cr); Dr Ajay Kumar Singh (ca, cb/Sunflowers). **Dorling Kindersley:** Twan Leenders (cb/Snake); The Natural History Museum, London (tc); Suhas Asnikar / Mangala Purushottam (c/Bonsai). **Dreamstime.com:** Adambowers (tl/Krakatoa); Igor Dymov (fcla); Sergey Uryadnikov / Surz01 (tl/Kelp Gull); Deymos (tc/Building); Cyberfyber (ca/Buildings, cb/Buildings); Tetiana Zbrodko / Ta (ca/Chrysanthemum); Demerzel21 (cr/Tower); Ongchangwei (cb). NASA AMES Research Centre: JPL-Caltech / T. Pyle (bc/Kepler). **NASA:** JPL / University of Arizona (br). **21 Dreamstime.com:** Andrey Sukhachev (cr). **Getty Images:** David Tipling / Digital Vision (tc). **22 Dreamstime.com:** Vhcreative (cla). **23 123RF.com:** tritooth (br). **Alamy Stock Photo:** Universal Images Group North America LLC / De Agostini Picture Library (cra). **Getty Images:** Wild Horizon (c). **24 123RF.com:** jupiter8 (bc). **Dreamstime.com:** Songquan Deng / Rabbit75 (ca). **24-25 Dorling Kindersley:** Simon Mumford / NASA (c). **25 123RF.com:** Michal Bednarek (ca); Vadim Nefedov (tl). **Alamy Stock Photo:** Overflightstock Ltd (bc). **Dorling Kindersley:** Simon Mumford / NASA (cr). **26 Dreamstime.com:** Anna Dudko. **26-27 Dreamstime.com:** Bennymarty (tc). **27 Getty Images:** Ed Reschke (cra). **28-29 Depositphotos Inc:** prudek. **29 Alamy Stock Photo:** WaterFrame (bl). **30-31 Getty Images:** Handout / U.S. Geological Survey. **32-33 Dreamstime.com:** Bennymarty. **32 Dreamstime.com:** Lasenby (bl); Minyun Zhou / Minyun9260 (cb). **34 Dorling Kindersley:** The Natural History Museum, London (crb). **35 Dreamstime.com:** Pklimenko (ca). **36 Dorling Kindersley:** The Natural History Museum, London (cb). **Dreamstime.com:** Kurhan (l). **36-37 123RF.com:** donatas1205 (Table). **37 Dorling Kindersley:** The Natural History Museum, London (crb). **Dreamstime.com:** Showface (bl). **38 Alamy Stock Photo:** Adam Eastland (tl). **Dorling Kindersley:** The Natural History Museum, London (tl). **Dreamstime.com:** Igor Kaliuzhny / Igorkali (cr). **38-39 Alamy Stock Photo:** Marshall Ikonography (c). **39 Alamy Stock Photo:** agefotostock Art Collection (cr). **40-41 Dreamstime.com:** Baluzek. **41 Alamy Stock Photo:** caia image / David Henderson (cla). **Dreamstime.com:** Mike7777777 (crb). **Getty Images:** Aaron Meyers. **43 Dreamstime.com:** Josemaria Toscano / Diro (ca); Anna Dudko (cla). **Getty Images:** Arterra (ca). **45 Alamy Stock Photo:** Stefan Sollfors (cra). **Dorling Kindersley:** The Natural History Museum, London (crb, cla). **46-47 Getty Images:** Timothy Allen. **47 Alamy Stock Photo:** Pavel Filatov (cr); Thomas Lehne (cra). **48-49 Getty Images:** Marianna Massey / Stringer. **48 Getty Images:** China News Service (br). **49 Alamy Stock Photo:** Organica (clb). **Getty Images:** Pone Pluck (br). **50-51 Dreamstime.com:** Mkos83 (b). **50 Alamy Stock Photo:** imageBROKER / Michael Szönyi (bl); Andrey Nekrasov (clb). **52 Alamy Stock Photo:** Newscom / BJ Warnick (ca). **Getty Images:** 1001nights (cl). **53 Alamy Stock Photo:** Everett Collection Inc (tc); KEYSTONE Pictures USA (ca). **54-55 Dreamstime.com:** Suwat Sirivutcharungchit. **55 Alamy Stock Photo:** David Fleetham (ca).

56 Dreamstime.com: Alextara (crb/Savannah); David Steele (tr); Demerzel21 (crb); Jonmanjeot (ca). **56-57 Dreamstime.com:** Christopher Wood / Chriswood44 (ca). **57 123RF.com:** SHS PHOTOGRAPHY (clb). **Dreamstime.com:** Naturablichter (c); Seaphotoart (ca). **58 Dreamstime.com:** Alessandro Zappalorto (clb). **Getty Images:** Ed Reschke (bc). **58-59 Dreamstime.com:** Littleny (bc). **59 Getty Images:** Joel Sartore, National Geographic Photo Ark (br); Reinhard Dirscherl / ullstein bild (clb). **60 123RF.com:** Songdech Kothmongkol (bl). **60-61 iStockphoto.com:** peeravit18 (c). **61 Alamy Stock Photo:** Nature in Stock / Jan van Arkel (ca). **Getty Images:** "Diane Cook, Len Jenshel" (bl). **Science Photo Library:** Dr. Richard Kessel & Dr. Gene Shih, Visuals Unlimited (tl); Eye Of Science (cb). **62 Alamy Stock Photo:** mauritius images GmbH / Reinhard Eisele (l). **Dreamstime.com:** Tamara Kulikova (b). **63 Dreamstime.com:** Natursports. **64-65 Alamy Stock Photo:** Bluegreen Pictures. **65 Dreamstime.com:** Andrey Armyagov (cra). **66-67 Alamy Stock Photo:** Grant Taylor. **66 Alamy Stock Photo:** Jason Wood Nature Photography (fclb); National Geographic Creative / Josh Humbert (clb). **Dreamstime.com:** Tamara Kulikova (fbl). **Getty Images:** Kryssia Campos (bl). **69 Dorling Kindersley:** Linda Pitkin (cra). **Dreamstime.com:** jeff waibel / Jfybel (ca); Natursports (cla). **70-71 Dreamstime.com:** Oleksandr Kotenko. **70 123RF.com:** Galyna Andrushko (clb); Łukasz Olszowiak (bl). **Dreamstime.com:** Eraxion (c). **72-73 Alamy Stock Photo:** Loetscher Chlaus. **72 Alamy Stock Photo:** imageBROKER / Hans Blossey (clb); mauritius images GmbH / Reinhard Eisele (bl). **74-75 Dreamstime.com:** Iuliia Kuzenkova. **74 NASA:** Provided by the SeaWiFS Project, NASA / Goddard Space Flight Center, and ORBIMAGE (clb). **75 NASA:** Jeff Schmaltz, MODIS Rapid Response Team (cla). **77 Dreamstime.com:** Alice Nerr (ca). **iStockphoto.com:** 13160449 (cra). **78-79 Getty Images:** Jeff Vanuga. **78 Dreamstime.com:** Achim Baqué (cra/Antarctica). **Getty Images:** Rick Price (cra/Ross). **80-81 Alamy Stock Photo:** Colin Harris / era-images. **80 Dreamstime.com:** Peregrinext (bl). **81 Alamy Stock Photo:** Tom Bean (cla); Ashley Cooper (cr). **Dreamstime.com:** Viktor Nikitin (cla/Ridge). **84 Alamy Stock Photo:** Solvin Zankl (cb/Lepidophanes Guentheri). **Dreamstime.com:** 111camellia (cb/Shark); Musat Christian (c); Harvey Stowe (bc). **Getty Images:** Joel Sartore / National Geographic (bc). **85 123RF.com:** Reto Kunz (cra/Noctiluca). **Alamy Stock Photo:** Nature Picture Library / David Shale (cra); NOAA (ca); Kelvin Aitken / VWPics (tc); Paulo Oliveira (cla/Mirrorbelly); Science History Images (bc). **Dreamstime.com:** Ppaula90 (tc/Jellyfish). **FLPA:** Norbert Wu / Minden Pictures (c, fcl/Black Swallower). **Science Photo Library:** British Antarctic Survey (cl/Sea-pig); Dante Fenolio (bl). **86 Getty Images:** JC Patricio (b). **86-87 Alamy Stock Photo:** Sputnik (t). **87 Alamy Stock Photo:** Gary Dublanko (cra). **88-89 NASA. 89 Alamy Stock Photo:** NASA Photo (c). **NASA:** Tony Gray and Sandra Joseph (cra). **90-91 Alamy Stock Photo:** Nawadoln Siributr (Used Thrice). **92 Alamy Stock Photo:** Mihai Andritoiu (cra, br). **93 Alamy Stock Photo:** All Canada Photos / Michelle Valberg (crb); Mihai Andritoiu (cla, clb). **Dreamstime.com:** Chuyu (b). **FLPA:** Ingo Arndt / Minden Pictures (cra). **94 Dreamstime.com:** Toniflap (bc). **iStockphoto.com:** narvikk (c). **95 Alamy Stock Photo:** Steve Gould / Stevegould (bc). **96-97 Alamy Stock Photo:** WILDLIFE GmbH (c). **96 Alamy Stock Photo:** World History Archive (c). **98 Dreamstime.com:** Les Cunliffe (tr); Jin Peng (cr); Isselee (crb). **100-101 Alamy Stock Photo:** Gary Dublanko. **102 Getty Images:** JC Patricio (clb). **102-103 FLPA:** Jim Brandenburg / Minden Pictures. **104-105 Getty Images:** Cultura RM Exclusive / Jason Persoff Stormdoctor. **104 Alamy Stock Photo:** US Air Force Photo (crb). **Dreamstime.com:** Sherah Martin (cra). **106 Dreamstime.com:** Narathip Ruksa / Narathip12 (tl). **106-107 Depositphotos Inc:** sunsinger (b). **107 Alamy Stock Photo:** Simon Belcher. **108-109 iStockphoto.com:** Starcevic. **108 123RF.com:** jpchret (clb). **Dreamstime.com:** Alena Shchipkova (bl). **110 Alamy Stock Photo:** North Wind Picture Archives (cl); John Vizcaino / Reuters (cb). **111 Dreamstime.com:** Janine Jeffery (bl); Sufi70 (tc). **112 Alamy Stock Photo:** Patrick Civello (c); Jamie Pham (br). **Hetch Hetchy Valley before construction of O'Shaughnessy Dam, M.M. O'Shaughnessy photograph collection, BANC PIC 1992.058--PIC, The Bancroft Library, University of California, Berkeley:** (bl). **113 Dreamstime.com:** Narathip Ruksa / Narathip12 (cla/Rice Fields). **iStockphoto.com:** OGphoto (br). **Library of Congress, Washington, D.C.:** LC-USZ62-128561 (bl). **114-115 Alamy Stock Photo:** Scott Wilson. **114 123RF.com:** Irina Pommer (tr). **115 Alamy Stock Photo:** Les Gibbon (cla). **116-117 Dreamstime.com:** Stockr. **116 Alamy Stock Photo:** Carolyn Franks (clb). **Dreamstime.com:** Tropper2000 (b). **117 Alamy Stock Photo:** Avalon / Photoshot License (br); B Christopher (cr). **118 Alamy Stock Photo:** Craig Leggat (c). **118-119 Dreamstime.com:** Andrii Hrytsenko (screen). **119 Alamy Stock Photo:** Ian Rutherford (tl). **120-121 iStockphoto.com:** luoman. **121 Alamy Stock Photo:** Paulo Oliveira (cra). **Dreamstime.com:** Aquanaut4 (b). **123 Getty Images:** J J D (br); jayk7 (c). **124 Alamy Stock Photo:** Daniel Dreifuss (c). **Getty Images:** Chris Johns / National Geographic (cla). **124-125 Alamy Stock Photo:** Tomasz Kowalski (bc); Genevieve Vallee (ca). **125 Alamy Stock Photo:** inga spence (cl). **Dreamstime.com:** Eric Isselee / isselee (br); Piotr Marcinski (crb). **128-129 Dreamstime.com:** Welcomia. **129 Dreamstime.com:** Stockphototrends (cl). **130 Alamy Stock Photo:** Simon Belcher (cra). **Dreamstime.com:** Vanja Terzic (br). **Getty Images:** Maher Attar / Sygma (c). **131 Alamy Stock Photo:** Stuart Aylmer (bl); View Stock (cla). **Dreamstime.com:** Artranq (cra/Girl); Daniel Prudek (cl); Magomed Magomedagaev / Forsterforest (cra/Cycling). **132 123RF.com:** tritooth (bc). **Dreamstime.com:** Musat Christian (bl). **133 Dorling Kindersley:** The Natural History Museum, London (br). **134 Dorling Kindersley:** Courtesy of Dorset Dinosaur Museum (cr). **134-135 Dreamstime.com:** Glasshoppah. **135 Dreamstime.com:** Bennymarty (b); Scol22 (tc). **134-135 Dreamstime.com:** lucentius (cb). **NASA:** NOAA / GSFC / Suomi NPP / VIIRS / Norman Kuring (ca). **136 Alamy Stock Photo:** Marshall Ikonography (l). **136-137 Dreamstime.com:** Glasshoppah. **137 Dreamstime.com:** Elena Duvernay (crb); Franz1212 (ca). **Getty Images:** by wildestanimal (bl). **140 Alamy Stock Photo:** Stefan Sollfors (crb). **U.S. Air Force:** (br). **143 Dorling Kindersley:** The Natural History Museum, London (bc). **Dreamstime.com:** David Steele (br).

Cover images: *Front:* **Dreamstime.com:** Titoonz; *Spine:* **Dorling Kindersley:** Linda Pitkin (sea star)

All other images © Dorling Kindersley
For further information see: www.dkimages.com